D1464467

Cover Illustrations:

Front Cover: The Commander's Cross of the Military St. Henry Order. The order was Saxony's highest award for distinguished military service and bravery in the face of the enemy.

Second Cover: The tunic of a *Flieger Leutnant* (Aviation Lieutenant) seconded from the *Verkehrstruppen* (Transportation Troop) with a replication of the awards that the Saxon ace, Max Immelmann, is wearing in the photograph on Page 26.

Third Cover: Aircraft profiles by artist Chuck Sterns depicting the markings of planes flown by four men who earned high Saxon awards for their exploits in the war. From top to bottom: Halberstadt D.V of *Oberleutnant* Hans-Joachim Buddecke, *Jasta 4*, October 1916. Albatros D.V of *Offizier-Stellvertreter* Paul Aue, *Jasta 10*, Summer 1917. Pfalz D. IIIa of *Hauptmann* Rudolf Berthold, *Jagdgeschwader 2*, April 1918. Fokker D.VII (Alb) of *Leutnant* Günther von Büren, *Jasta 18*, September 1918. Markings data by Dan-San Abbott.

Fourth Cover: Max Immelmann and Fokker D.III 246/16 as portrayed by aviation artist James Dietz. As a leading *Eindecker* exponent, Immelmann earned the sobriquet *"Der Adler von Lille"* ("The Eagle of Lille"). He was killed in this machine on June 18, 1916.

By the Same Author

Aviation Awards of Imperial Germany in World War I
Volume I - The Aviation Awards of the Kingdom of Bavaria

Aviation Awards of Imperial Germany in World War I and the Men Who Earned Them
Volume II - The Aviation Awards of the Kingdom of Prussia

AVIATION AWARDS OF IMPERIAL GERMANY IN WORLD WAR I
And the Men Who Earned Them

Volume III - The Aviation Awards of the Kingdom of Saxony

Neal W. O'Connor

Foundation for Aviation World War I
Princeton, New Jersey

Copyright 1993 by Neal W. O'Connor
Published in the United States by the Foundation for Aviation World War I
Princeton, New Jersey 08542

Typesetting and Graphics by
Walsworth Publishing Company, Inc.

Printed and Bound in the United States by
Walsworth Publishing Company, Inc.

ISBN 0-9619867-0-2 (v.3)

Library of Congress Cataloging-in-Publication Data
O'Connor, Neal W. 1925 -
Aviation Awards of Imperial Germany in World War I and the Men Who Earned Them
Bibliography: p.
Contents: v. 3 The aviation awards of the Kingdom of Saxony
1. Germany - Armed Forces - medals, badges, decorations, etc.
2. Aeronautics, Military - Germany - History - World War, 1914-1918
I. Title
UG1185.G3026 1993   358.4'11342'0943   87-38144
ISBN 0-9619867-0-2 (v. 3)

Contents

"An accident - he shot his own propeller off! He was unconquered! How fine for him that he found such a swift and beautiful soldier's death!"

Quote on the death of Max Immelmann by a comrade, Oswald Boelcke

Author's Preface And Acknowledgements

Those who have read either of the first two volumes in this series will be familiar with, but hopefully not yet tired of, the approach used here. It is an attempt to show how a frequently complex system of military awards in the Imperial Germany of World War I was used to motivate the young men who fought the first full-scale war in the air and how they were used to reward bravery that was often of a very high order.

The first two volumes covered the awards to airmen emanating from the Kingdoms of Bavaria and Prussia. The next most important entity after them in the 2nd *Reich* of 1871 was the Kingdom of Saxony and so it was logical that its awards became the focus of this third volume. The original intent was to include the awards of the Thüringian States, eight smaller dominions located close to the western boundries of Saxony. But as the work grew, it became clear that the awards of Saxony provided enough subject matter to fill a single volume and those of these other states should await the next effort.

As before, much help has been received from many individuals and institutions which is gratefully acknowledged. Four names need to be singled out for special thanks however. First and foremost is A. Edward Ferko of Salem, Ohio. Once again he has opened his vast archive and photographic library to support this effort, providing invaluable information not available elsewhere and images that in many cases are unique. Similarly, Eric C. Ludvigsen of Arnold, Maryland once more gave the author the benefit of his firm grasp of the intricacies of the Imperial German States' awards system, offering advice and adding details the author would have overlooked. George A. Seymour of Plano, Texas greatly aided the on-ground research done at the *Staatsarchiv* in Dresden and his help in this respect will also be evident when the awards of the Thüringian States are covered in a future volume in this series. Jerry J. Siano of Newtown, Pennsylvania designed and laid out the first of these books and the style he set has been continued here. All four of these men are owed a large debt as are the many others who knowingly, and sometimes unknowingly, helped including, especially, Peter M. Grosz of Princeton, New Jersey, Alex Imrie of Harpenden, England, Peter Kilduff of New Britain, Connecticut and Manfred Thiemeyer of Zülpich, Germany.

The photographs used herein are vital in bringing the awards and the men who earned them to life and much is also owed to those who have generously allowed pictures and documents in their possession to be reproduced here. They include Richard A. Baumgartner, the Berlin Museum for Transportation and Technology, the Dresden Military History Museum, A. Edward Ferko, Peter M. Grosz, the late Rudolf Hannemann, Margot Hemer, Hertha Höhne, Alex Imrie, the late Erwin Jollasse, Peter Kilduff, *Dipl.-Ing.* Karl Kössler, *Dr. Volker Koos*, Hans H. Munte, the late Heinz J. Nowarra, the late William R. Puglisi, George A. Seymour, Bruno J. Schmäling, Noel C. Shirley, *Dr. Dr.* Holger Steinle, Manfred Thiemeyer, George H. Williams and H. Hugh Wynne.

All material used on the color covers of the book as well as most of the awards and documents illustrated in black and white are from the collection of the Foundation for Aviation World War I.

Lastly, as always, it needs to be said that all errors and omissions are entirely the responsibility of the author. As the last chapter in this book entitled "Errata and Addenda" attests, he is quite capable of making his full share of them despite all the help he has received.

Neal W. O'Connor

Princeton, New Jersey

The Kingdom of Saxony

The heart of the territory that comprised the latter-day Kingdom of Saxony was the old March of Meissen. The term "Saxony" had migrated there from the medieval Duchy of Saxony (so-named after its original inhabitants, the Saxons). The Duchy, which broke up in 1180, occupied the middle reaches of the Elbe and the Wesser, north and west of Meissen. A portion of the old Duchy in its south-easternmost corner was called Wittenberg. When in 1425 (some accounts say 1423) the Emperor Sigismund gave the Electoral Duchy of Saxe-Wittenberg to Friedrich, Margrave of Meissen as a reward for Friedrich's defense of Imperial interests during the Hussite wars (the ruling line had died out in Wittenberg), "Saxony" became associated with the House of Wettin. Friedrich's grandsons, Ernst and Albert, partitioned their territories in 1485, thereby founding the Ernestine and Albertine Lines of the House of Wettin. The Ernestine line was considered the senior but in 1547 its head, Johann Friedrich the Magnanimous, was forced to sign the Capitulation of Wittenberg whereby the electoral dignity was transferred to the junior Albertine line. In the latter half of the 16th Century, the Electorate of Saxony prospered and after the Hapsburg dominions themselves, was considered the next most important realm in the Empire. Saxony's involvement in the Thirty Years War after 1631 was, however, a disaster. It was plundered by friend and foe alike and nearly a century would pass before the damage was repaired.

Not helping the situation was the man who ruled as Elector of Saxony from 1694 to 1733. He was Friedrich August I, known as "The Strong." And "strong" he was, not only physically but also in his appetite for food, drink and women (it is said that when he died, he left 354 bastard children and that at least one of his illegitimate daughters became his mistress at one time). His interests included art and architecture and his extravagances in these areas, plus the costly Polish wars, nearly bankrupted Saxony even as its capital,

Dresden, was becoming one of the most beautiful and civilized cities of its day. Friedrich August I was elected the King of Poland in 1697, changing his name to August II as well as his religion. Up to that time, all the Electors of Saxony were Protestant but he converted to Catholicism on ascending the throne of Poland. This produced the unusual situation of a succession of Catholic rulers in Saxony, a land that was predominately Protestant. August II was deposed as King of Poland in 1704, formally resigned the crown in 1706 but was reinstated in 1709. He died in 1733 and was succeeded by Friedrich August II, his only legitimate son. The new Elector was also named King of Poland the same year and crowned in January 1734. He inherited his father's love of the arts, so much so that he left the affairs of state to his minister, *Graf* von Brühl. Von Brühl was an incompetent who involved Saxony in two Silesian wars and the Seven Years War. In the latter conflict, with Friedrich August and von Brühl safely sitting it out in Poland, Saxony itself was again laid waste. Both men returned to Dresden after the conclusion of the Seven Years War but, happily for Saxony, both died in 1763.

Friedrich Christian, Friedrich August's oldest surviving son (two brothers ahead of him had died, one as a baby and the other as a youth age six), became the next Elector but only survived his father by two months. Next in line was Friedrich Christian's son, Friedrich August, who was only 13 years old. Until he reached his majority, his mother, a Bavarian princess, acted as Regent. Under Friedrich August, who ruled as Friedrich August III and became known as "the Just," a period of reckoning for the excesses of his great-grandfather and grandfather set in. The huge debts incurred by them were gradually reduced and under economic reforms, agriculture and businesses began to flourish again. When in 1791 an offer was made that he, too, ascend the throne of Poland, which was to be made hereditary and not elective if he accepted, Friedrich August, mindful of the trouble the crown

Das Deutsche Reich (The German Empire) of 1871-1918. *Sachsen* (Saxony) can be located just over the *Österreichisch-Ungarische Monarchie* (Austro-Hungarian Monarchy) border with its three principal cities of Dresden, the capital, Leipzig and Chemnitz.

had brought to Saxony, wisely turned it down.

Even as Friedrich August was putting the affairs of Saxony on the home front in order, his vacillations in the power struggles of the time produced dire results for Saxony. Napoleon was on the march, threatening all of Europe and Friedrich August at first attempted to keep Saxony neutral. Failing at this, he put his armies into the field as allies of Prussia and suffered defeat along with them at the Battle of Jena in 1806. Napoleon offered an olive branch and Friedrich August took the bait, abandoning Prussia in the process and retreating into the neutrality he had first sought. After the Peace of Posen and the establishment of the Confederation of the Rhine, he threw in with Napoleon completely. With the promised contribution of 20,000 Saxon troops Friedrich August not only joined the Confederation but accepted the further enticement of a more exalted title. On December 11, 1806, the same year that Saxony committed itself to the Confederation, he became King Friedrich August I of Saxony.

In the following year he was further rewarded with the title of Grand Duke of Warsaw and other Polish territories were added to his new kingdom. Again he vacillated, however, after Napoleon's disastrous Russian campaign in which his troops took part. In 1813 he flirted with the idea of an alliance with Austria. But Napoleon's victory at Lützen put him squarely back in the French camp. As a consequence, Saxony was invaded by the allies and Friedrich August was forced to flee to Prague. At the critical Battle of Leipzig in 1813 Napoleon was checked and the Saxon troops in one of those switches not considered remarkable at the time went over to the allies. For a brief period Friedrich August found himself a prisoner. During his captivity Saxony was first governed by the Russians and then the Prussians. At the Congress of Vienna in 1814 and 1815, where the victorious Austrians, Prussians and Russians wrestled with the remaking of the map of Europe following Napoleon's final defeat, the fate of Friedrich August and his lands were hotly debated. Russia was all for handing all of Saxony over to the Prussians on the condition that it, in turn, receive Prussian-held Poland. Austria wanted nothing to do with that proposition since taking all of Saxony would have put Prussia right on its own borders. In the end, Prussia did take about two-thirds of the Saxony that was not contiguous with Austria. What was left was handed back to Friedrich August and the chastened

king was allowed to keep his crown. He died in Dresden on November 15, 1828.

Friedrich August's successor, King Anton I, ruled from 1827 until his death in 1836. The signal event in his reign were the uprisings in Leipzig and Dresden in the revolutionary year of 1830 which followed the July Revolution in Paris. As a result of these disturbances Anton was forced to promulgate a constitution and accept his nephew, Friedrich August II, as co-regent (Friedrich August's father, Maximilian, younger brother of Anton and Friedrich August I had renounced his right of succession; he died in 1838). Friedrich August II ruled alone after Anton's death until his own death in 1854. There were further stirrings of constitutionalism and revolution in Saxony during his time. They peaked in 1849 and were suppressed with the assistance of Prussian troops. The next king was Johann I. He was a scholarly and learned man but he, too, managed to choose the wrong side when an aggressive and expansion-minded Prussia under its "Iron Chancellor," Otto von Bismarck, decided in 1866 to rid itself once and for all of Austria's ambitions to remain a German power. The German Confederation had made Berlin and Vienna competing power centers within Germany proper. There was never a question that Austria was, had been and would remain a great power; only whether it would be a German power or a Danubian one.

Bismarck prepared his ground well. He secured the neutrality of France, which would be dealt with later, and the friendship of Italy. Alarmed, Austria created a coalition which Saxony joined along with Bavaria, Hanover and the Hesses (Hesse-Darmstadt and Hesse-Kassel). The war that ensued can thus be called a German civil war. The conflict itself was sharp, short and decisive. It ended with the crushing one-day defeat of Austria at Königgrätz, also known as the Battle of Sadowa, on July 3, 1866. Bismarck dissolved the German Confederation and at Prague where a treaty of peace was concluded in August of 1866, Italy was rewarded with Venetia from Austria and Prussia annexed the Kingdom of Hanover and the Duchies of Hesse-Kassel and Nassau as well as the Free City of Frankfurt. Prussian troops occupied Saxony and while it was not forced to cede any territory this time, Saxony was made to pay huge reparartions for its perfidy. Bismarck created a new North German Confederation and Saxony dutifully joined. Only the heavily Catholic south of Bavaria,

King Albert of Saxony (left) who ruled from 1873 until 1902 and King Friedrich August III (right) the last King of Saxony. Albert is wearing the Grand Cross of the Military St. Henry Order from a special collar created for him in 1893 on the occasion of his 50th anniversary of military service. At the neck is his Grand Cross of the 1870 Iron Cross which he earned on March 22, 1871 when Crown Prince of Saxony. His was one of only nine Grand Crosses of the Iron Cross awarded for the War of 1870. Friedrich August III came to the throne in 1904 following a two year reign by Albert's brother, Georg. The Grand Cross of the Military St. Henry Order that he is wearing is a special Grand Master's badge, made even larger than it already was by the addition of ball-tips on the points of the cross. It is believed that this was also a one-off and worn only by Friedrich August III.

Württemberg and Baden remained completely independent of Prussia. Austria was excluded from any further German affairs and with that, the Hapsburg's vision of a Greater Germany in which it would play a leading role disappeared forever.

Bismarck was now free to turn to the real enemy, France. War broke out in 1870 after an adroitly fostered exchange of calculated insults to national pride, that traditional excuse for hostilities between rival powers. France was likewise soundly defeated after a series of bloody battles and Germany occupied France for two years (and Paris for one day). This stunning victory convinced the remaining German states to throw in with Prussia and the other members of the North German Federation to form one nation under Prussia's domination. In 1871 in the Hall of Mirrors at Versailles the new German Empire was proclaimed. A reluctant Wilhelm I, King of Prussia, was persuaded by Bismarck to become the German *Kaiser*. The harsh terms of the peace treaty called for an indemnity of two billion francs but what really rankled was the annexation of Alsace and Lorraine which became Imperial German Domains. Thus were the seeds sewn for revenge and retribution that only another war between France and Germany could satisfy.

The Saxon dynasty would see three more monarchs before the collapse of the German Empire in the aftermath of World War I. Albert I ruled from 1873 until 1902. As Crown Prince, Albert had distinguished himself as a general officer in the field, first on the Austrian side against Prussia in 1866 and then on the Prussian side against France in 1870. Albert's brother, Georg, had only a brief tenure on the throne, from 1902 until 1904. The last Saxon king was Friedrich August III, a large rather homely man, plain spoken but kind. It was he who saw his people through the early triumphs and later tragedies of World War I. On November 13, 1918, following the Armistice, he was forced to renounce his throne and Saxony became a Free State. Nonetheless, he remained well-liked by his former subjects who genuinely mourned his death in 1932.

Background

German military aviation was only in its infancy on the eve of World War I although considerable progress had been made since October 1, 1913 when the office of *Inspektion der Fliegertruppe (Idflieg)* was established for the organization and fielding of mobile aviation units. When mobilization orders went out in the early evening hours of August 1, 1914, the strength of the *Fliegertruppe* consisted of:

— 30 *Feldflieger-Abteilungen* under Prussian control having a complement of six aircraft each. These were numbered one through 30.
— Three *Feldflieger-Abteilungen* under Bavarian control, each with six aircraft also. These were numbered one through three. To distinguish them from their Prussian counterparts, they carried the designation *"b"* after the unit number.
— Nine *Festungsflieger-Abteilungen* under Prussian control for the six fortress towns and the three permanent military bases numbered one through nine and one under Bavarian control numbered one.[1]
— Eight *Ettapen Flugzeugparke* for the supply and replacement of both men and equipment for flying units in the field.
— Five *Flieger-Ersatz-Abteilungen* that also supplied the mobile flying units with personnel and equipment. These replaced the five pre-war *Flieger-Bataillone*.

A sixth *Flieger-Ersatz-Abteilung* came into being when *FEA 6* was established at Grossenhain in Saxony on December 1, 1914. Its first commandant was *Major* von Winckwitz. A number of men who later were among Germany's most successful fighter pilots started their aviation careers there or later trained at this base. This included the premier fighter pilot of the war, the 80-victory ace, Manfred *Freiherr* von Richthofen. He attended the observer school at Grossenhain from June 10, 1915 until June 21 when he was posted to his first combat aviation detachment, *Feldflieger-Abteilung 69*, on the Russian Front.[2]

At the start of the war, there was only one aviation unit that was identified as Saxon. This was *Feldflieger-Abteilung 24* (later, in the reorganization of the *Fliegertruppe* that occurred in late 1916/early 1917, it was converted to *Flieger-Abteilung (A)264*, the *(A)* indicating a unit assigned to artillery cooperation duties). Subsequently, either later in their existence or upon formation, 10 two-seater flights and seven *Jagdstaffeln* were designated Saxon. Similarly, Bavaria and, to a lesser extent, Württemberg had their own aviation units.[3]

---

[1] Two of these, both Prussian, never materialized because of transport and aircraft problems and existed only on paper.

[2] Among other aces who trained at Grossenhain early in their aviation careers were the following men who, like von Richthofen, went on to earn Prussia's highest bravery award for officers, the famous *Orden Pour le Mérite* (victory scores in brackets after each name): Julius Buckler (36), Carl Degelow (30), Walter Blume (28), Kurt Wüsthoff (27), Rudolf Windisch (22), Hans Berr (10) and Ernst *Freiherr* von Althaus (9). Another who trained at Grossenhain was the 18-victory ace, Hartmut Baldamus, a Saxon. He was killed on April 14, 1917 in the process of scoring his final victory. Had he been able to add just a few more victories, he would have been a candidate for the *Pour le Mérite*, the requisite number of victories before a man was considered for the award being about 20 at the time. More details on his career appear later in the book.

[3] None of the lesser German states was ever assigned aviation units. Those not designated Saxon, Bavarian or Württembergian remained Prussian. However, in late 1917 (possibly early 1918) the Grand Duke of Baden, Friedrich II, with a burst of nationalistic pride let it be known that it was his royal wish to have all-Badener aviation units too. It might have been all right if he merely wanted the designation only but no, his proposal was that the some 1,134 native Badeners then serving in the *Fliegertruppe* be transferred to form self-contained units (while eventually the Bavarian units came to be staffed with natives of that kingdom and non-Bavarians transferred out, the Saxon and Württembergian formations

Those units carrying Saxon designations comprised the following:

Original Designation and Later Designation(s)	Date of Saxon Affiliation
FFl.Abt. 24 - Fl.Abt. (A)264	Saxon unit upon mobilization for war
FFl.Abt. 29 - Fl.Abt. (A)278	Date unknown
FFl.Abt. 54 - Fl.Abt. 24 - Schusta/Schlasta 38	Date unknown
FFl.Abt.60 - Fl.Abt. (A)275	November 24, 1917
FFl.Abt. 66 - Fl.Abt. 34	November 24, 1917
Art.Fl.Abt. 204 - Fl.Abt. (A) 204	November 24, 1917
Art.Fl.Abt. 208 - Fl.Abt. (A) 208	November 24, 1917
Art.Fl.Abt. 226 - Fl.Abt. (A)226	November 24, 1917
Art.Fl.Abt. 231 - Fl.Abt. (A)231	November 24, 1917
Fl.Abt. (A)244	Date unknown
Fl.Abt. (A)250	November 24, 1917
Jasta 21	November 24, 1917
Jasta 22	November 24, 1917
Jasta 24	November 24, 1917
Jasta 40	December 11, 1917
Jasta 44	January 1, 1918
Jasta 54	February 11, 1918
Jasta 72	

Source: *Flieger-Formationen*

Something should be said at this stage about *Feldflieger-Abteilung 23*, later *Flieger-Abteilung 23*, because, as we shall see, so many of its men received high Saxon decorations. While officially it was a Prussian unit, it seems to have had close connections with Saxony. In fact, in some reference sources and on various medal rolls where a man's unit is listed, it is referred to as a Royal Saxon contingent.

With this very brief background, the stage is now set to discuss the awards of the Kingdom of Saxony and the airmen who received them during the First World War. The highest order in the land was the House Order of the Rue Crown.[4] It had been founded in 1807 by King Friedrich August 1, called "the Just," whose initials, "F A," appeared prominently on the obverse center medallion of the badge. Like many of the highest orders of knighthood and chivalry, it came in only one class and automatically carried with it a breast star of the usual eight-pointed, silver-rayed type. It was meant for Saxon Royalty, especially meritorious natives and foreigners of the highest ranks and stations and for friendly foreign rulers and princes. As such, it was well beyond the reach of the young officers who fought in World War I regardless of the degree of bravery or the level of perseverance they displayed. The badge was a pale green enameled maltese cross edged in gold and white which was worn from a broad grass-green sash. The motto of the order, *Provi/Dentiae/Memor* ("Mindful of Providence"). was displayed on three lines on the center medallion of the star. Since the order had no application to the men in this study, we can go on to those Saxon awards that were open to the airmen (and others) during the war.

Befitting its position as a powerful state, Saxony had a number of other honors for those who rendered valuable service but whose station precluded them from consideration of the Rue Crown (whose

---

contained a majority of men from other places for the most part). *Idflieg* protested to the War Ministry, pointing out the serious interruption of operations that such a move would entail (and this on the eve of the last big German push of the war which was designed to knock out the British and French before the full weight of the American effort could be felt). The Grand Duke's scheme would have required the units so stripped of Badeners to find equally skilled personnel elsewhere, a commodity in very short supply in the last year of

the war in Germany. Fortunately for the German war effort, nothing ever came of the hair-brained idea.

[4] Webster defines "rue" as a strong-scented shrub with bitter leaves. In the arms of the cross there were four ornamentations in gold resembling a ducal coronet, the trefoils representing the Chaplet of Rue (or the Rue Crown). The trefoil design was also carried around the center medallion on both the badge and breast star.

exclusivity in any case had to be protected). There were three lesser orders and a string of crosses and medals. Of these, the most prestigious was the Military Order of St. Henry which, as the name implied, was strictly an award for serving officers, either for conspicuous personal bravery on the battlefield or, in the case of officers of higher rank, more frequently than not far removed from any physical danger itself, for merit in positions of great responsibility. As a gesture of friendship and consistent with the courtesies of the times, the order in its higher classes was also bestowed on the royalty of other principal German states and the three nations allied to Germany in World War I. There was a Gold Medal and a Silver Medal associated with the order. These were the officer's counterpart awards and were meant for deserving non-commissioned officers and men.

Next in line was the Merit Order which with the

additional embellishment of a pair of crossed swords to indicate an award for military performance was used to recognize bravery and merit during the war.[5] It, too, had an enlisted man's counterpart, in this case a cross. At the end of the orders scale was the Albert Order. Not surprisingly, it was the most commonly awarded of all three orders. There was an associated cross for the troops here as well. Finally, there was still another cross and two medals, one in silver and the other in bronze, that were also available for distribution among non-commissioned officers and men on combat status. Obviously, then, Saxony did not lack for honors to bestow upon its deserving sons and others serving its cause during the war. This included the young men who fought the first full-scale war in the air and it is to those awards and the stories of the airmen who won them that we now turn.

---

[5] Upon the foundation of the order in 1815 its legal name was the "Civil Merit Order." This was explicitly changed to the "Merit Order" in Paragraph 1. of the Statute Amendment of September 24, 1849.

The Military St. Henry Order

Of the five great military orders of Imperial Germany, the Saxon Military St. Henry Order was the oldest. It was founded on October 7, 1736 by Augustus III, King of Poland and Elector of Saxony. It thus preceded such famous awards as the Prussian *Orden Pour le Mérite* (founded on June 6, 1740), the Württemberg Military Merit Order (founded on February 11, 1759 as the Ducal Württemberg Military Order of Carl), the Bavarian Military Max-Joseph Order (founded on June 8, 1797) and the Baden Military Karl-Friedrich Merit Order (founded on April 4, 1807).[1]

The Military St. Henry Order originally came only in one class as an award for merit by officers of the Royal Saxon Army. The order was enlarged when three classes were established by Elector Friedrich August III in 1768. These were Grand Cross, Commander and Knight. In 1829 King Anton divided the Commander grade into a Commander 1st Class and a Commander 2nd Class (the distinction being that the Commander 1st Class carried with it a breast star; the badges were the same for both Commanders). At the time of this division, all then existing Commanders were automatically deemed to be holders of the 1st Class.

The color illustrations show the appearance of the Commander's and Knight's badges which were in use at the time of World War I so it is only necessary to mention a few points about the insignia that are otherwise not apparent. All the badges were identical except for size. As was the custom, the Grand Cross was the largest of all with the Commander and Knight badges being proportionately reduced versions. Since the breast stars that accompanied the Grand Cross and Commander, 1st Class grades had no application

to the fliers of World War I, they will not be described in detail. Suffice to say both were of the usual eight-pointed type with the Commander's, 1st Class star being a bit smaller than the Grand Cross star.

The manner of wear of the badges was dependent on grade. The Grand Cross was worn at hip level suspended from a broad sash. Although not specifically sanctioned in the statutes (unlike the Prussian Crown Order and the Red Eagle Order where the matter was spelled out), it also became the practice in less formal situations to wear the Grand Cross from the neck. There was also a special collar from which the Grand Cross badge was worn. But this was a unique award, made especially for King Albert on October 24, 1893 to mark the 50th anniversary of his entering military service. Also worn from the neck were the Commanders' badges. The Knight's badge, hereafter called the Knight's Cross, was worn either suspended from its ribbon looped through a buttonhole on the front of the tunic or pinned on its ribbon on the upper left breast in conjunction with other earned breast badges. When worn with other awards in the latter manner, each from its appropriate ribbon, the assemblage was called the *Grossordensschnalle* (literally, the "large orders bar"). Often, especially in everyday service situations, the actual insignia of the Knight's Cross was not worn at all. Its presence among a man's honors was merely indicated by its ribbon, again either looped through a buttonhole of the tunic or by a reduced version of the ribbon on a small bar on the left breast. This small bar was called the *Feldschnalle* (literally, the "field bar"). The ribbon was the same for all grades, a pleasing combination of pale blue with yellow-gold stripes near each edge, the military colors of Saxony.

---

[1] The Ducal Württemberg Military Order of Carl died out in the 1780s, was revived in 1799 and went through some other permutations before emerging as the order which existed at the time of World War I.

The figure on the center medallion on the obverse of the badges and breast stars was that of the order's patron, Heinrich II, the last Saxon Emperor (1002-1024), who was later canonized. What cannot be seen in the photographs of the order is the reverse side of the badges. These carried the order's motto *Virtuti In Bello* ("Bravery in War") on a blue enamelled riband in the center of which were the arms of Saxony, a green chaplet of rue placed diagonally on a field of horizontal black and gold bars.

The number of awards of the Military St. Henry Order in World War I testify to its exclusivity. By grade they were as follows:

Grand Cross	12
Commander, 1st Class	14
Commander, 2nd Class	153
Knight's Cross	2,717

Source: *Der Königlich Sächsische Militär-St. Heinrichs-Orden 1736-1918*

Note: A researcher writing for a German orders and medals journal has listed the names of 11 more men who were said to receive the Knight's Cross of the order in addition to the 2,717 listed in the standard reference source cited above. Nine of these 11 awards were made after the Armistice. Of these, the latest bestowal date was January 27, 1921. None of the 11 awards was to an airman. Many of the surnames appear to be Jewish and it is possible that these recipients were expunged from the roll of the order during the Hitler regime and were never properly reinstated afterwards.

During World War I the Grand Cross of the order was as a matter of course bestowed on the Saxon king and as a matter of courtesy, to the sovereigns of the other three kingdoms in the German Empire and to the rulers of the three nations allied to Germany in the war. The awards to three other German royals were of a more substantive nature because they held high military ranks and commanded armies in the field (albeit

perhaps only nominally as in the case of the German Crown Prince after the failure at Verdun in 1916). The list of the 12 recipients of the Grand Cross included the two senior army commanders as from August 29, 1916 until the end of the war. In order of actual or probable receipt they were:

— King Friedrich August III of Saxony on October 21, 1914
— Emperor Wilhelm II of Germany, King of Prussia on October 22, 1914
— Emperor Franz Joseph I of Austria (no known date but probably 1914-1916)
— Czar Ferdinand of Bulgaria (no known date but probably 1914-1916)
— Sultan Mohammed V of the Ottoman Empire (no known date but probably 1915)
— General Field Marshal Prince Leopold of Bavaria on October 23, 1916
— General Field Marshal Paul von Hindenburg on December 27, 1916
— King Ludwig of Bavaria on January 27, 1917
— King Wilhelm II of Württemberg on January 29, 1917
— General Field Marshal Crown Prince Rupprecht of Bavaria on May 7, 1918
— General of Infantry Crown Prince Wilhelm of Germany on May 7, 1918
— General of Infantry Erich Ludendorff on May 7, 1918

One of the important provisions of the order was that there would be promotion through the grades, i.e., a man had to start with the Knight's Cross, then progress to the Commander and, finally, to the Grand Cross. The governing words in Paragraph IV of the 1829 Statues read: "Grand Crosses will be chosen from Commanders and Commanders from the Knights, and no Knight will be promoted to a higher grade who has not occupied the lower grade." This progression might not have applied to someone like the Kaiser who received the Grand Cross in the first instance.[2] There was sufficient authority for such an exception. Further wording in the 1829 Statutes said: "In cases of especially distinguished service to the person of the King or to the troops, or on account of 50 years of exemplary service, We reserve to Ourselves and Our Successors the right

[2] However, when the Grand Cross of the Military St. Henry Order that belonged to Czar Ferdinand of Bulgaria was recently auctioned along with many of his other orders, also present was a Knight's Cross of the order. So at least in this

instance, the regulations about normally being a Knight of the order were apparently observed. Undoubtedly, both were presented at the same time.

to make an exception, upon due consideration, to the above rules concerning promotion to the next highest grade of the order."

For most, though, it was necessary to hold the Knight's Cross and one of, but not necessarily both of, the Commander's grades before the Grand Cross was possible. There was a way to speed this process up for especially distinguished recipients. Both a Knight's Cross and one of the Commander's grades could be awarded simultaneously. Thus did von Hindenburg receive both the Knight's Cross and the Commander, 1st Class on December 21, 1914. Similarly, Prince Leopold of Bavaria was awarded the Knight's Cross and the Commander, 2nd Class together on February 9, 1916. From there, both would then progress to the Grand Cross later on. Of interest is the fact that the German Crown Prince made the full progression through all of the four grades of the order, from the Knight's Cross on November 23, 1914, to Commander, 2nd Class on November 19, 1915, to Commander, 1st Class on May 4, 1917 and finally to the Grand Cross on May 7, 1918.

As the previous table indicated, the Commander, 1st Class was awarded almost as sparingly as the Grand Cross. Of the 14 recipients, four were royals holding military rank and the remaining 10 were distributed to Germany's most senior and distinguished leaders in the field. The (relatively) more liberal use of the Commander, 2nd Class served to recognize other men of General officer rank and field grade officers. Only a handful of awards of the Commander, 2nd Class went to junior officers. Interestingly, there was not a navy man among any of the recipients of either the Commander, 1st Class or 2nd Class. The 153 awards of the Commander, 2nd Class broke down by the following army ranks:

Royals holding military rank:	4
General officers:	46
Colonels:	28
Lieutenant Colonels:	24
Majors:	41
Captains:	9
Senior Lieutenants:	0
Lieutenants:	1

The only airman-recipient of the Commander, 2nd Class was the lone Lieutenant. His story, and the reason for his exceptional recognition, will be presented shortly.

Before turning to the awards of the Knight's Cross during the war, and where the airmen begin to figure in more prominently, two additional points concerning the administration of the order ought to be mentioned. First, the insignia of all grades of the order were to be returned to the Orders Chancery upon the death of the recipient. Likewise, on promotion to a higher grade, the insignia of the lower grade were also to be turned in. The language of Paragraph XIII of the 1829 Statues spelled this out: "Orders insignia will be returned to the Orders Chancery upon death, and upon promotion to a higher class." On September 15, 1915, however, an amendment modified this with the provision that upon promotion to a higher grade, the Knight's Cross was to be retained and worn. Effectively, then, this called for only the Commander's insignia to be turned in in the (unlikely) event of promotion to the Grand Cross. Secondly, all rules were off after the end of World War I. Without the monarchy around, most recipients naturally chose to retain their insignia. There were a few widows and other surviving family members who did return a deceased's insignia for which they received a small cash bonus.

One final note. When Knights of the order had reason to wear their crosses in later years at reunions and other formal occasions, it became the custom to wear their badges at the neck, on a cravat as one would wear the Commander's badge. By this time, of course, they were long out of uniform and in civilian dress this manner of wear was much more appropriate (although some still preferred to wear their full *Grossordensschnalle* to display all to which they were entitled).

Of the total of 2,717 awards of the Knight's Cross of the Military St. Henry Order (or a total of 2,728 if the additional 11 awards mentioned earlier are added), 107 of them went to airmen for their exploits in aerial action (see Appendix II for a list of recipients in order of receipt, Appendix III for a list arranged alphabetically and Appendix IV for a list according to the type of flying unit in which the award was earned). In comparison to the Knight's Crosses of the other four important military orders of Imperial Germany, the St. Henry Order in absolute numbers was possibly the most frequently distributed overall (see disclaimer below) and definitely the second most frequently given within the air services. A rather different picture emerges, however, if the awards to fliers are

The Knight's Cross of the Military St. Henry Order (left), Saxony's highest honor for bravery on the battlefield, mounted on its draped ribbon. The pale blue color of the ribbon with its narrow lemon-yellow side stripes, the military colors of Saxony, has been all but washed out in this photograph. Of the more than 2,700 Knight's Crosses that were awarded for World War I, only 107, or about four percent, went to officers in aviation contingents.

This *Grossordensschnalle* (large orders bar) shows a line-up of awards that represent those which several Saxon fliers earned during the war. The first three comprise the "Saxon Trio," these being the Knight's St. Henry followed by the Knight 2nd Class with Swords of the Merit and Albert Orders. Following these are the Prussian Iron Cross, 2nd Class and the Knight's Cross with Swords of the Royal Hohenzollern House Order. Native Saxons (and native Bavarians too) wore their home state's bravery awards ahead of those of Prussia, Everyone else, regardless of being Prussian or not, wore Prussian bravery awards first.

examined as a percentage of all Knight's Cross awards during this time. On that basis, Saxony allotted the second smallest percentage of the total of the five orders involved to airmen. These points are made in the following table:

State	Awards of the Knight's Cross in WW I	Total Awards	Aviation Awards	Percent Aviation
Baden	Military Karl-Friedrich Merit Order	288	8	2.8
Bavaria	Military Max-Joseph Order	246	11	4.5
Prussia	*Orden Pour le Mérite* [1]	687 [2]	76	11.1
Saxony	Military St. Henry Order	2,717	107	3.9
Württemberg	Military Merit Order	2,170 [3]	156 [3]	7.2

Sources: Baden - *Generallandesarchiv* Karlsrühe

Bavaria - *Virtuti pro Patria - Der königlich Bayerische Militär-Max-Joseph-Orden*

Prussia - *Geschichte Der Ritter Des Ordens Pour le Mérite im Weltkrieg - Band I und II*

Saxony - *Der Königlich Sächsische Militär-St. Heinrichs-Orden 1736-1918*

Württemberg - *Die Württemberger im Weltkriege*

The statutes of the Military St. Henry Order specified that "this military order is meant only for commissioned officers in the service of the King of Saxony, from the highest to the lowest rank, without distinction of faith, noble birth or length of service. Only merit, as displayed in the field, linked with loyalty to King and Fatherland, can open the door to this order." These restrictions were similar to those governing the award of the highest bravery order of most of the other German states. They, too, tended to restrict them to natives or others performing some direct service to the state. Only Prussia, because of its pre-eminent position in the Empire, felt called upon to award its *Orden Pour le Mérite* (and its Iron Cross and Royal Hohenzollern House Order) throughout all contingents and regardless of a man's birth. The following table shows that almost all aviation recipients of the Military St. Henry Order had some connection with Saxony, either by birth or through service to the state:

Aviation Recipients of the Knight's Cross of the Military St. Henry Order

	Number	Percent
Saxon-born recipients	63	59
Non-Saxons with commissions in the Royal Saxon Army	16	15
Non-Saxons with previous service in Saxon ground contingents	15	14
Non Saxons serving in Saxon aviation contingents	9 [4]	8
Non-Saxons with no direct connection with Saxon military service	4 [5]	4
Total	107	100

Source: *Der Königlich Sächsische Militär-St. Heinrichs-Orden 1736-1918*

---

[1] The term "Knight's Cross" in reference to the *Pour le Mérite* was not generally used although recipients were called knights of the order.

[2] In addition, there were 122 awards of the Orden *Pour le Mérite mit Eichenlaub.* No flier in the war received the order with Oakleaf (although Manfred von Richthofen was, unsuccessfully, proposed for it). For that reason, these 122 awards have not been included in the tabulation.

[3] These numbers include only native Württemberger recipients or men who were serving in Württemberger contingents at the time of their award. Thus they are unquestionably understated to some degree.

[4] This number includes four non-Saxons who were serving in *Feldflieger-Abteilung 23* at the time of their award. As noted, although the unit was not officially designated a Saxon contingent, it was often listed as one and for the purpose of this tabulation has been considered as such.

[5] The four men were *Rittmeister Prinz* Friedrich Sigismund

The formal bestowal document (left) to the Military St. Henry Order carrying the signature of King Friedrich August. This is the one issued to the later 44-victory *Pour le Mérite* ace, Rudolf Berthold, who received the Knight's Cross on April 8, 1916.

The typewritten certificate (below) dated after the Armistice confirming the award of the Knight's Cross of the Military St. Henry Order to Karl Höhne, an observer then serving in *Flieger-Abteilung (A)248* when he earned the order on October 29, 1918.

One other small statistic might be of interest. A number of fliers held both a *Pour le Mérite* and a high bravery order from either Baden, Bavaria, Saxony or Württemberg. But only one airman had the *Pour le Mérite* and more than one of these other top bravery orders, another demonstration of just how restrictive these other four states were in passing out their highest orders to men of other states or to those not in their own service. Fittingly, the flier who was the exception was Germany's premier fighter pilot, Manfred von Richthofen. He also held the Knight's Cross of the Württemberg Military Merit Order in addition to his Knight's St. Henry mentioned above. From Baden he received no recognition whatsoever even though it had two orders that ranked below its Military Karl-Friedrich Merit Order which could be awarded for bravery.[3] However, he came very close to also having Bavaria's highest bravery award, the Military Max-Joseph Order. In May 1917 the Prussian authorities made application to the Orders Chancery in Munich that von Richthofen be so recognized. The Bavarians turned the proposal down on the basis that von Richthofen, a Prussian, was not one of their own people. However, such an important hero of the Fatherland could not be ignored completely, even by the chauvinistic Bavarians who never did like taking instructions from their haughty (to them) Prussian brothers. In a compromise von Richthofen was awarded the Bavarian Military Merit Order, 3rd Class with Crown and Swords. If von Richthofen felt slighted (and there is no indication anywhere that he was), he should not have been. No other flier in the war, even the 11 Bavarians who earned the Max-Joseph Order for aerial action, ever progressed beyond the 4th Class grade with Crown and Swords, two steps below von Richthofen's award (there was a 3rd Class grade with Swords only).

All of the aviation awards of the Knight's Cross of the Military St. Henry Order were to men of junior officer rank.[4] The majority, as expected, went to the younger *Leutnante,* the most common rank among the German officer-airmen. The distribution was:

Rank When Awarded the

St. Henry Knight's Cross	Number	Percent
Lieutenants	66	62
Senior Lieutenants	28	26
Captains	13	12
Total	107	100

The year-by-year distribution of the awards of the Knight's Cross of the Military St. Henry Order shows an interesting pattern. One would think that the numbers would be skewed toward the later war years when aerial activity was at its height and more men were engaged in the service. Such was not the case with this order. Nearly as many Knight's Crosses were awarded to airmen in the first three years of the war as were given afterward. Quite the opposite was true in the case of the aviation award of the other four military orders that we have been examining. There the numbers bulked up in 1917, 1918 and in the immediate post-war period when some retrospective awards were made and back-dated to 1917 and 1918. This was especially true of the *Orden Pour le Mérite.* Fully 83 percent of the aviation awards of the "Blue Max" were made in 1917 and 1918 (no retrospective awards were made after the Armistice and the *Kaiser's* abdication).[5] The year-by-year pattern of the awards of these five orders, using the same sources as those in the earlier table showing the break-down between the total of Knight's Crosses awarded and those going to airmen only, is shown on the first table on the next page. The second table makes the comparison of the combined years 1914, 1915 and 1916 versus 1917, 1918 and the post-war period.

---

of Prussia, the then *Oberleutnant* Manfred *Freiherr* von Richthofen, *Leutnant* Wilhelm Baumbach and *Leutnant* Walter von Bülow. As also noted earlier, von Richthofen had undergone observer training at *Flieger-Ersatz-Abteilung 6,* a Saxon installation at Grossenhain, however.

[3] These were the exclusive Order of Berthold I. (only 23 Knight's Crosses awarded in World War I) and the much more widely distributed Order of the Zähringen Lion (7,549 Knight's Crosses awarded during the war).

[4] It should be noted that the Commanding General of the Germany Army Air Service, *Generalleutnant* Ernst von Heppner, received the Knight's Cross of the order on October 21, 1914. At the time, however, he was Chief of Staff of the 3rd Army.

[5] See the last chapter entitled "Errata and Addenda" for the author's speculation as to how this term, the "Blue Max," came about.

<u>Distribution of Awards of Knight's Crossess of Premier Bravery Orders of Five German States</u>
<u>To Combat Airmen</u>
<u>by Years</u>

State	Award	1914	1915	1916	1917	1918 and Post-War	Total
Baden	Military Karl-Friedrich Merit Order	--	1	2	1	4	8
Bavaria	Military Max-Joseph Order	--	1	1	0	9	11
Prussia	*Orden Pour le Mérite*	--	--	13	25	38	76
Saxony	Military St. Henry Order	7	18	23	36	23	107
Württemberg	Military Merit Order [1]	4	22	38	59	33	156

	Awarded in 1914, 1915 and 1916		Awarded in 1917, 1918 and Post-War		Total Awarded for World War I	
State	No.	Percent	No.	Percent	No.	Percent
Baden	3	38	5	62	8	100
Bavaria	2	18	9	82	11	100
Prussia	13	17	63	83	76	100
Saxony	48	45	59	55	107	100
Württemberg [1]	64	41	92	59	156	100

Why Saxony, in relative terms, was so liberal with awards of the Knight's St. Henry Order to airmen so early on in the war has no ready answer. One would have thought that the Albert and Merit Orders would have largely sufficed for at least the first two or three years of the war and that during that time the St. Henry would come into play only in exceptional cases. That was certainly the case in Prussia. There were no aviation awards of the *Orden Pour le Mérite* until early 1916. And before that, there were just several (perhaps as few as two) awards of the Knight's Cross with Swords of the Royal Hohenzollern House Order to fliers. For the rest, the Iron Cross in the 1st and 2nd Classes sufficed in the early years of the war. Whatever may be said about Saxony's apparent eagerness to recognize its air heroes almost from the beginning (the first such award was on November 11, 1914), it was a lot more equitable than Prussia in spreading around its highest bravery order to all branches of the air service. Prussia, on the other hand, went overboard in favoring the fighter pilots with its *Pour le Mérite*.[6]

The following table shows the distribution of the Knight's St. Henry by type of aviation unit. It can clearly be seen that the men in the workhorse two-seater squadrons garnered the majority of the awards, as well they should have doing as they did the really valuable work in the air - reconnaissance and artillery fire direction being the most important with bombing probably next

[1] As noted on an earlier table, these numbers include only native Württembergers or men who were serving in Württemberg contingents at the time and consequently are understated to some degree.

[6] Of the 76 awards of the *Orden Pour le Mérite* to airmen in combat, 48 of them went to men serving in a *Jagdstaffel* at the time. Additionally, there were 11 awards to men acting as fighter pilots in the early *Feldflieger-Abteilungen* before the *Jasta* were formed. Three naval fighter pilots also received the award. Thus 62 out of the 76, or nearly 82 percent, were accounted for by fighter pilots.

although close-in infantry support, a later development, would have assumed a much bigger role had the war continued.

in the entire German Air Service. However, Immelmann was the 22nd airman to have earned the award up to that time so that alone would not

Distribution of Aviation Awards of the Knight's Cross of the Military St. Henry Order, 1914-1922, by Type of Unit

Feldflieger-Abteilungen	38 [1]
Flieger-Abteilungen (A)	28
Jagdstaffeln	12 [2]
Flieger-Abteilungen	8
Artillerie-Flieger-Abteilungen	5
Kampfgeschwadern der O. H. L.	5
Bombengeschwadern der O. H. L.	3
Marine	2 [3]
Schutzstaffeln	2
Brieftauben-Abteilung-Ostende	1 [4]
Flieger-Ersatz-Abteilungen	1 [5]
Gruppenführer der Fliegern	1 [6]
Schlachtstaffeln	1
Total	107

There is no question about who was the most famous aviation recipient of the Military St. Henry Order. And for once we are not talking about the redoubtable Manfred von Richthofen who so often rates top billing when it comes to any discussion of the air awards of Imperial Germany. The man in this case was Max Immelmann. As a _Leutnant_ he was awarded the Knight's Cross of the order on October 13, 1915 a few days after he had scored his fourth confirmed victory. This was a remarkable feat for that early period in the air war and it tied him with another exponent of the Fokker _Eindecker_, Oswald Boelcke, for top scoring honors

have been enough to give him the title of the order's most famous aviation recipient. What does give him that distinction is the fact that he was the lone _Leutnant_ of the war, and the only air officer, to be decorated with the order in the grade of Commander, 2nd Class. Additionally, so far as available records have shown, only one other airman held an order in a grade equivalent to that for service at the front although, in fairness, it should be mentioned that two other famous fighter pilots came close to matching Immelmann's achievement.[7]

[1] Three recipients were serving as fighter pilots flying Fokker and Pfalz _Eindeckers_ in _Feldflieger-Abteilungen_ at the time of their awards.

[2] One recipient was serving in a _Jasta_ at the time of his award but it came for his service in a two-seater unit.

[3] Both recipients served in two-seater seaplanes.

[4] This was actually a two-seater bombing unit later designated _Kampfgeschwader Nr. 1 der O.H.L._ on December 20, 1915.

[5] The recipient earned his award for service in a two-seater unit.

[6] The recipient earned his award for service in a two-seater unit.

[7] The airman who equalled Immelmann's high honor was _Hauptmann_ Erich Suchsland of _Feldflieger-Abteilung 60_. He

received the Schwarzburg Honor Cross, 3rd Class with Swords on March 27, 1915. This was a breast badge equivalent of a Knight's Cross. There was also a 2nd Class badge which was worn on the breast too. According to records obtained at the _Staatsarchiv_ in Rudolstadt, one of the two seats of the principality (the other was at Sondershausen), the same _Hauptmann_ Suchsland, still in _Feldflieger-Abteilung 60_, received its Honor Cross, 1st Class with Swords on August 16, 1915. This was a badge worn at the neck and can be considered a Commander's badge. The archive had no futher information on the details of this award and why, if deserving of further recognition, he jumped over the 2nd Class of the order which, in the normal course of things, would have been the next logical step.

Oberleutnant Immelmann †
(letzte Aufnahme)

610
Postkartenvertrieb W. Sanke
BERLIN N. 37.

Max Immelmann in full dress at the peak of his fame and glory. At his neck is the Commander's badge of the Military St. Henry Order. Below that and off to side is his *Pour le Mérite*. Immelmann, as a Saxon, put a higher value on his Commander's badge and, as seen here, wore it in a superior position to his Prussian award. His order bar, reading from left to right, displays all his German states' awards save one. They are: the Knight's Cross of the Military St. Henry Order, the Knight 2nd Class with Swords of the Albert Order, the Friedrich August Medal in Silver, the Iron Cross, 2nd Class, the Knight's Cross with Swords of the Royal Hohenzollern House Order, the Bavarian Military Merit Order, 4th Class with Swords and the Hamburg Hanseatic Cross. Missing is the Anhalt Friedrich Cross, 2nd Class which he must have received after this formal studio pose was taken. It is believed this photograph was made soon after the bestowal of the Commander's badge on March 31, 1916. It shows him while he was still a *Leutnant*.

The two fliers who very nearly earned an award on the same plain as Immelmann's Commander's St. Henry were (as one might expect) Manfred von Richthofen and a highly decorated Bavarian, Adolf *Ritter* von Tutschek.

To mark the occasion of his 70th aerial victory which occurred on March 26, 1918, von Richthofen was proposed for the Oakleaf to his *Pour le Mérite*. This would have been a signal honor, easily on a par with any Commander's badge if not considered even superior (and certainly so by the Prussians). Some stickler in the Orders-Commission in Berlin turned down the idea, falling back on the archaic language of the statutes which called for a recipient of the Oakleaf to the *Pour le Mérite* to have either captured a fortress, successfully defended one or won a battle. It was pointed out that von Richthofen had done none of these things (when Ludendorff later heard of the decision, he is said to have snorted, "Richthofen has won many battles!"). Instead, von Richthofen was awarded the Prussian Red Eagle Order in a grade quite high for his rank, the 3rd Class (there was a lower 4th Class) and in a rare and near unique-for-World-War-I combination, with both Crown and Swords. As a breast badge, and strictly speaking, it was not quite on a par with the Commander's grade of an order (as, say, the Red Eagle Order, 2nd Class would have been).

Von Tutschek earned the right to his personal nobility and the addition of *"Ritter* von" to his name when he received the Knight's Cross of his native state's highest bravery order, the Military Max-Joseph Order, on January 31, 1916. It came for his heroic performance as an infantry company commander the previous summer on the Eastern Front. He had led an assault against a Russian position and then held it for 17 days against repeated counter-attacks until he was relieved. Returning to the Western Front, he was gassed at Verdun in 1916 and, like many of his peers, took the occasion of his convalescence to apply for a transfer to the air service. By August 1917 he was in command of *Jasta 12* and had 21 confirmed victories to his credit. On the 3rd of that month he was notified of the award of his *Pour le Mérite*. Eight days later, he was seriously wounded in the arm in combat with a Royal Naval Air Service triplane. While in his hospital bed, the officer in charge of all aviation units in the area told him that his name was being put in for the Commander's Max-Joseph. Everyone was optimistic that it would be forthcoming. In the

event, nothing ever came of the proposal nor was it acted upon after his death in action on March 15, 1918. Had it been approved, it would have been a rare event. There were only 21 awards of the Commander's grade of the order during the war and only one of these was to a junior officer (a posthumous award to a 22-year old *Leutnant* and storm troop commander).

Max Immelmann's war began in fairly uncertain fashion and gave no hint of the great things that were to come. As a reservist, he was called to the colors two weeks after the conflict broke out. He was ordered to report to his old unit, the 2nd Railway Regiment. As a brand new product of the Dresden Cadet School, he had joined this unit in 1911 as a *Fähnrich*. He found little satisfaction with the transport service in those pre-war years. Even an interim stint at the War Academy at Anklam did nothing to convince him that a permanent military career was for him. However, one event while at the War Academy left a profound impression. During a tour of various army facilities at the end of 1912, a stop along the way was the military airfield and installation at Johannisthal near Berlin. There the mixed bag of Farmans, Rumplers and Wright aircraft were paraded for the young officers-to-be and several were flown. Wrote Immelmann, "one seldom sees anything so splendid."

Back in the routine of his old regiment again, Immelmann became convinced that he should resign in order to pursue more practical work. This he did and started studies at the Technical High School in Dresden. He devoted himself to his tasks taking particular interest in the technical aspects of motorcycles and automobiles and their engines. When war was declared, Immelman was, like most of his generation all over Europe, eager to see active service but he was not very enthusiastic about the prospects of this if it meant returning to his old unit. So when he read that the Inspectorate of Aviation was seeking volunteers to be trained as pilots, and not yet having his call-up orders, both he and a younger brother, Franz, immediately applied. Those with mechanical training were to be given preference and Max and Franz undoubtedly embellished their credentials in the forms they had to fill out. But nothing was heard of the matter when shortly thereafter, on August 18, Max had his orders to rejoin his old outfit. Three months of dull garrison duty in Berlin followed while the war's first momentous battles raged in France and Belgium on the Western Front and on Germany's eastern boundaries. But Immelmann's application had not been in vain and while the prospects for a quick and decisive German victory in the west had faded by November, his own took a decided turn upward when he was ordered to report to *Flieger-Ersatz-Abteilung Adlershof,* also in Berlin. He arrived there on November 12. Next door was the military aviation school at Johannisthal, the same installation where his interest in flying had first been whetted two years before. After a couple of weeks of flights with an instructor, Immelmann could say, "flying is splendid."

Bad weather around the turn of the year slowed the progress of the eager young pilots-to-be but when another period of fair weather set in, Immlemann was allowed to solo. Altogether, he had made 54 training flights before he took the controls alone. Before he could qualify as a military pilot and hope for a frontline assignment, he, like others, had to pass a series of three tests which included a number of prescribed maneuvers, landings and cross-country flights. Earning the right to wear the silver badge of a pilot of the Imperial German Army Air Service was no quick and easy matter. But even before Immelmann could complete all his courses he was ordered to report to *Armee-Flugpark 3* in early March 1915. Here was progress! This aviation supply depot was located at Rethel, northeast of Reims. He was getting closer to the front at last. There, at the end of the month, he finished his formal training although his final flight was not without incident. He and his observer lost their way in low clouds and had to put down in a forced landing when their fuel ran out. The touchdown went smoothly but in taking off in the late afternoon to return to home base after having secured a new fuel supply, a gust of wind caught the aircraft as it was taxiing and the undercarriage was damaged. This repaired, they finally got back to Rethel two days later, but not without difficulty. The air was very rough and the numbing cold caused Immelmann to make a less than perfect landing although no further damage was incurred. Such were the hazards of simply flying in those early years.

On April 12 Immelmann left the peace and quiet of Rethel behind with orders to report to *Feldflieger-Abteilung 10* at Vrizy. He flew his own machine to his new assignment, full of anticipation

of action at last. He was up the very next day on a familiarization flight with an observer to point out the ground they would cover. On landing, however, Immelmann again made a rough landing and the undercarriage was wiped out. Sheepishly, he had to return to Rethel to pick up a replacement. On getting back to Vrizy with the new aircraft, he very nearly botched another landing. Again there was undercarriage damage but this time it could be quickly repaired. The next days found him on regular artillery spotting missions over the lines, at least one of which proved to be eventful. On this occasion his aircraft was heavily archied and in dodging the bursts, Immelmann got into a dangerous sideslip. After a scary fall of over 1,500 feet, he managed to regain control however and complete the mission.

Immelmann's stay at *Feldflieger-Abteilung 10* was short lived. He found himself transferred to a new field aviation section, *Feldflieger-Abteilung 62,* which had been formed on April 23. The unit's Commanding Officer was *Hauptmann* Hermann Kastner, a qualified pre-war flier. Immelmann took up his new posting on April 28. One of his fellow pilots there was *Leutnant* Oswald Boelcke. By the standards of the time he was a veteran. He had had seven months of service at the front, coming from *Feldflieger-Abteilung 13.* He had been decorated with the Iron Cross, 1st Class. This award would lose much of its prestige as the war ground on but in the first year of the war it was noteworthy recognition. Together, Immelmann and Boelcke would form a strong bond of friendship even as a friendly rivalry developed while they forged careers as Germany's most formidable fighter pilots of their day and which had many remarkable parallels. *Feldflieger-Abteilung 62* moved to its operational base at Douai, south of Lille and opposite the British in front of Arras. As soon as men and equipment were settled in and the aircraft assembled, the routine work of artillery spotting and photographic missions began in their L.V.G.s. [8] The enemy planes they would face carried machine guns but the only armament the German B-Type aircraft could rely on were carbines and pistols, not likely to do serious damage to their adversaries although probably good therapy for the aggressive German air crews.

Immelmann soon found out the disadvantages of

---

[8] A product of Luft-Verkehrs G.m.b.H. (literally "Air Traffic Company, Limited"), a large aircraft manufacturer located at

the Johannisthal airfield near Berlin.

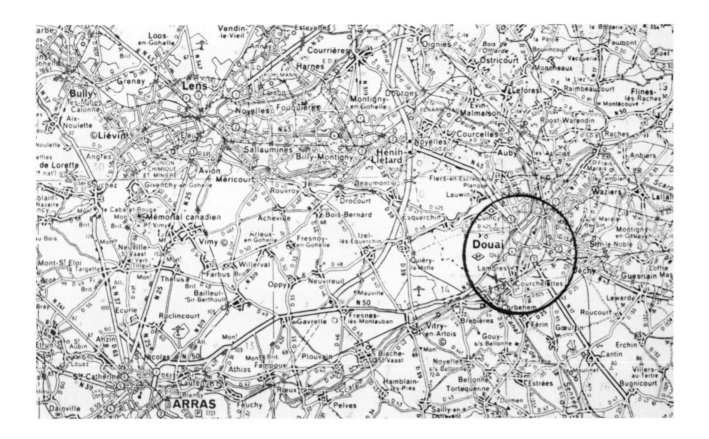

Douai, the home of *Feldflieger-Abteilung 62* (circled in the map above), was 15 miles northeast of Arras and 12 miles southeast of Lens. Off this map lay Lille, 19 miles to the north. The actual air strip of *FFl.Abt. 62* was just outside of Douai proper, at La Brayelle (circled in the map below).

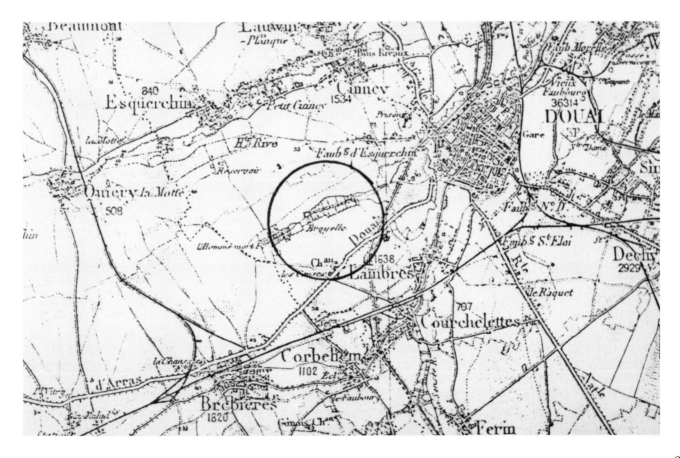

this situation. On June 2 he had his first taste of aerial combat and had to rely on a ruse to escape. He and his observer, *Leutnant* Ehrhardt von Teubern, were out on a photo ops when they were attacked by an armed enemy plane. Each time the hostile aircraft made a run at their plane, Immelmann went right after him as though they also carried a machine gun which von Teubern could bring to bear. Each time the enemy plane turned away and finally left them alone whereupon Immelmann and von Teubern coolly completed their mission. The next day things were even more hot. Flying with von Teubern again, they were again attacked. This time their opponent was even more determined. While von Teubern continued to expose his plates, they were twice raked with machine gun fire. At last their job was completed and they could make a break for Douai which they reached safely. About a half dozen shots from the enemy plane had gone harmlessly through the wings of their L.V.G. but one had grazed a strut. Had that hit it squarely and broken it, there could have been a disaster. These first experiences of combat also coincided with Immelmann's first military decoration. On June 4, the day after the second action, *Hauptmann* Kastner presented the young Saxon with the Prussian Iron Cross, 2nd Class.

It was not long before *Feldflieger-Abteilung 62* developed a sting of its own. An armed enemy plane had been forced down not far from the Douai aerodrome and Kastner managed to appropriate the French machine gun it carried. This was mounted on the fastest of the unit's L.V.G.s. Naturally, as the pilot with the most seniority, Boelcke took it over. Then a factory armed C-Type aircraft finally reached the unit.[9] Boelcke moved up to this mount and Immelmann inherited the improvised L.V.G. Even then, Immelmann was considered the next best pilot to Boelcke, or at least the next most aggressive, and so Kastner made the assignments on that basis. On the first flight across the lines with their new C-Type plane on June 15, Boelcke and his observer, *Leutnant* Heinz Helmut von Wühlisch, reported an engagement with the enemy and on the next day had three separate brushes. The last of these was in the evening ending at 8:50

p.m. after some one hour and 15 minutes, a very long time for any aerial duel. In each of these three instances one of the machines, all identified as French, was seen to go down but no definite results were observed and no claims were made for a decisive victory. Immelmann, too, was now engaging in regular combats with his armed L.V.G. He had tinkered with the gun mount and felt he had repositioned it to give his observer the best chance of a success. On his second flight with it, a Frenchman put a bullet in its gas tank and that fate most feared by airmen, being "shot down in flames," was a real possibility. Fortunately, the gas merely leaked out and Immelmann was forced to make a hurried landing. In another encounter, he and his observer drove two enemy planes back to their own lines but whether any positive results had been obtained was, again, impossible to determine. More and more it appeared that the honor of scoring *Feldflieger-Abteilung 62's* first confirmed victory was going to be a toss-up between Immelmann and Boelcke at the rate things were going. In the end, the nod went to Boelcke.

But before that momentous event, an aircraft that would markedly change the fortunes of both Immelmann and Boelcke had arrived at the front. It was the nimble-for-its-time new product of the Dutch aircraft designer who was employed by the Germans, Antony Fokker. And the plane, of course, was the Fokker *Eindecker*. In itself, from the E.I through the final E.IV production models, it was no big improvement in the state of the art. What made it special, and gave it its notoriety (e.g. "The Fokker Scourge") was that it carried a fixed Spandau machine gun synchronized to fire through the arc of the propeller via an interrupter gear that prevented (in theory) bullets from shattering it.[10] As such, it was specifically designed for air combat. Fokker himself arrived at Douai to demonstrate it. Boelcke took it up for the first time on June 24. But Boelcke was still using his two-seater for operational missions when he and his observer scored *Feldflieger-Abteilung 62's* first confirmed victory.[11] On July 4 he was up with von Wühlisch again when a French Morane Parasol two-seater monoplane flew over them at a greater

---

[9] Possibly the aircraft was Albatros C.I 162.15

[10] The E.I and E.II as well as most of the E.IIIs carried only one gun. A few E.IIIs were fixed with two and Immelmann tried one out with three guns which, because of the excess weight, was not successful. The E.IVs had two guns but here,

too, the weight of a heavier two-row rotary engine and the guns were too much for improved performance.

[11] In the German scoring system, as in other countries, both members of a two-seater crew were given credit for a victory regardless of who fired the shots.

Immelmann and his observer, von Keller, in an L.V.G. C.I of *Feldflieger-Abteilung 62* sometime in mid-1915. This machine is possibly 32/15 which was initially flown by Oswald Boelcke and then inherited by Immelmann when Boelcke was assigned the factory-armed 150 hp. L.V.G. 162/15. Boelcke flew this latter aircraft from June 14, 1915 on until he switched exclusively to the first of *FF1.Abt. 62's Eindeckers.* It was in 162/15 that Boelcke scored his first victory on July 4, 1915 when he and his observer, *Leutnant* Heinz Helmut von Wühlisch, were credited with a Morane two-seater.

height. They managed to catch up with it and after about 20 or 25 minutes had ensued, Boelcke got into a position so that von Wühlisch could bring his gun to bear. Von Wühlisch's fire, some 83 rounds in all, took effect. The enemy plane first went into a glide, with Boelcke pursuing, and then nosed over and fell into a deep wood in German-held territory. Boelcke put their plane down in a nearby meadow and by the time they reached the crash site, the wreckage had already attracted a large crowd. Papers on the bodies of the French crew showed that by a quirk of fate one of them was the Count de Rochefocault whose family owned the very estate where the wood stood. Both airmen had multiple bullet wounds and Boelcke was sure they had been killed in the air. The victory produced an immediate award of the Iron Cross, 1st Class for von Wühlisch. Boelcke, already possessing it, had to settle for the congratulations showered on them by their comrades and for the Army and Corps communiques that mentioned their feat.

Perhaps as a further reward, Boelcke took over the *Eindecker* and from July 7 flew it exclusively. Immelmann inherited the two-seater in which the July 4 victory had been scored. Once again he seemed to be in the shadow of Boelcke but if he were a bit disappointed in still another hand-me-down, it didn't show in his writings. On the contrary, he expressed delight in the fact that he would from now on not have to be as much on the defensive as he had been. And, indeed, his job was an offensive one, flying protection for the unit's still unarmed two-seaters as they performed their missions. In quick succession, two rewards of his own came in recognition of his good work. On July 15 he received the Saxon Friedrich August Medal in Silver and on July 20 he was promoted to *Leutnant der Reserve*.[12] The latter news came via telegram in the middle of a birthday party for *Hauptmann* Kastner and was made effective as from July 14.

On July 30 Immelmann got what appears to have been his first chance to try out the *Eindecker* himself. After watching Boelcke handle the controls, he took it up and, according to him, made five perfect landings in succession. Boelcke thought otherwise and wrote that, actually, Immelmann seemed to have great difficulty in

landing well. Whichever version was correct, what happened two days later proved that Immelmann was a fast study. By now there were two *Eindeckers* on strength at *Feldflieger-Abteilung 62* and while he was first in line to use the second one, Immelmann was still expected to undertake two-seater missions. Accordingly, he was scheduled for just such a job on the morning of August 1 but was sleeping in because the weather was bad. However, it wasn't bad enough for the enemy apparently. Just about dawn an English formation appeared over the aerodome and commenced bombing. Not at the ready, it was too late for anyone at *Feldflieger-Abteilung 62* to get up into the air in an effort to intercept them. But when a bit later it was reported that either this force or another was on their way back for what looked like another strike, both Immelmann and Boelcke rushed to the field to get up into the air. Boelcke was off in his *Eindecker* and although he wasn't able to catch up with the new intruders, he did fasten on to what he identified as another French monoplane. He had his opponent cold when he suffered a jam. There was nothing he could do to clear it so he had to break off the action and return to have the problem fixed. Initially, Immelmann had intended to take off in his two-seater for his part in the action. His observer, however, felt it was useless because of the poor visibility and refused to go along. Immelmann then returned to the second *Eindecker*. Calling himself "not a lazy man," he had the Fokker wheeled out of its hanger and took off for his first solo combat mission.

The time elapsed must have been very short because he caught up with Boelcke and saw him attacking his intended victim. Then he observed Boelcke diving away, not knowing, of course, of Boelcke's gun stoppage and thus fearing the worst. It was too late for Immelmann to go after this quarry but between Douai and Arras he caught up with what he thought was another French plane which had just dropped its bomb load on Vitry. There were two more enemy planes above him so he had to be careful and act quickly. This he did and forced his intended victim into a left-hand turn, taking him in the opposite direction of the safety of his own lines. Immelmann, too, experienced several jams but managed to clear them and continue to shoot. The "Frenchman"

---

[12] The Friedrich August Medal, which came in Silver and Bronze, was an award meant for non-commissioned officers and men but could also be awarded to men with the rank of

Fähnrich. Immelmann obviously just squeaked by in receiving this award since as a *Leutnant*, he would not have been eligible for it.

Immelmann's friendly rival in *Feldflieger-Abteilung 62* was the equally
famous Oswald Boelcke. Here he is shown in a Fokker E.IV in 1916.

Machine gun practice in *Feldflieger-Abteilung 62*. At the gun is *Hauptmann* Ritter and awaiting their
turn are, left to right: von Wühlisch, Boelcke, Porr, von Teubern and Immelmann.

went into a steep glide but got down intact. Immelmann landed next to his victim and was surprised to find only one occupant of what turned out to be a B.E.2c of No. 2 Squadron, RFC.[13] He was lightly wounded in the left arm and had flown without an observer so that the plane could carry a heavier bomb load. Until the usual crowd had gathered (this being behind German lines) and a doctor found, Immelmann rendered first aid and the pair conversed politely. The Englishman complimented Immelmann on his shooting which, indeed, had been very good. It was something of a miracle that the British pilot had not been more seriously wounded or killed. The aircraft had taken some 40 hits and much of it, including the instrumentation, was shot to pieces. Back at the aerodome Boelcke offered his sincere congratulations. Privately, he was annoyed however. He had been flying his *Eindecker* for nearly a month without any result and when at last a target presented itself, his gun had jammed.

Immelmann, in a gesture typical of the day, flew an L.V.G. all the way to St. Pol and back, a round trip of some 70 miles, to drop a note to the British telling of the loss of one of their planes and the fate of the occupant. On the next day, August 2, Immelmann was notified that his victory had earned him immediate recognition. The congratulatory message from the Commanding General in the area closed with these words:

> "I herewith express to *Leutnant* Immelmann my high appreciation of this gallant deed and confer upon him in the name of his Majesty our Emperor and King the First Class of the Iron Cross.
>
> von Pritzelwitz."

There now began the friendly rivalry between Immelmann and Boelcke referred to earlier, with first one scoring a victory and then the other but with Boelcke usually just a step ahead. Boelcke got his first kill on an *Eindecker* on August 19 for number two over-all. Immelmann pulled even on September 10 when he forced two enemy planes down, one of which crashed and was confirmed. Again there was immediate recognition for the feat. The same day he learned that he had been awarded the Knight's Cross, 2nd Class with Swords of the Saxon Albert Order. Immelmann thought it "a charming order." Boelcke was also in line for another medal at this time. It could properly be called one of the most unusual awards ever going to a German airman because of the circumstances that earned it. On August 28 Boelcke had rescued a 14-year old French lad from drowning in a canal that ran in front of *Feldflieger-Abteilung 62's* mess. The grateful townspeople actually wanted the French government to award him its legion of Honor which, upon hearing about it, Boelcke thought was a great joke. Kastner took the matter seriously too and put in Boelcke's name for the Prussian Life Saving Medal which, in due course, was approved.[14]

The two men each scored a victory in September with Boelcke again just a step ahead of Immelmann. Boelck'e third came on September 18 and Immelmann celebrated his 25th birthday by matching Boelcke's performance on the 21st. The day after that Boelcke was notified of an abrupt transfer to Metz where he was to join *Brieftauben-Abteilung-Metz*.[15] The prospect of his leaving *Feldflieger-Abteilung 62* just as things were going so well did not please him at all. But as the old German soldier's saying goes, *"Befehl ist Befehl"* ("orders are orders") and he dutifully left for his

---

[13] He was 2/Lt. William Reid.

[14] The medal itself was not presented to Boelcke until December 11, 1915 when Kastner handed it to him upon Boelcke's return to *Feldflieger-Abteilung 62*. It had just arrived in the squadron mail, not an uncommon method of delivering even the highest awards although a formal investiture was certainly the preferred method if circumstances permitted. Thereafter, Boelcke proudly wore its yellow-gold and white ribbon looped through a buttonhole directly under the black and white "war ribbon" signifying the Iron Cross, 2nd Class and on which he also wore a small gilt crossed swords and crown device to indicate the Knight's Cross with Swords of the Royal Hohenzollern House Order by which time he had received. All Prussian breast awards employed the black and white ribbon when awarded for bravery thus some sort of device was necessary to distinguish

the prestigious Hohenzollern Knight's Cross from the more lowly Iron Cross.

[15] *Brieftauben-Abteilung-Metz* was the second of two units then using cover names. The other was *Brieftauben-Abteilung-Ostende*. BAO (as it was frequently termed) had been formed to carry out attacks on England. When bases close enough to put its aircraft within operational range could not be secured before the German advance of 1914 was checked, *BAO* then carried out conventional work on the Western Front. It had been formed on November 27, 1914 and *BAM* followed on August 17, 1915. On December 20, 1915 *BAO* was designated *Kampfgeschwader Nr. 1* and *BAM* became *Kampfgeschwader Nr. 2*, these being considered more appropriate terms for units like them and the three new ones that also were established on the same date.

The still smoldering wreckage of Immelmann's third victory, B.E.2c No. 2004 from No. 10 Squadron, RFC, on September 21, 1915. It came down between Acheville and Willerval and burst into flames upon crashing. Mercifully, the pilot, 2/Lt. S. W. Caws, whose grisly corpse can be seen in the right foreground, was killed in the air. The observer, Lt. W. H. Sugden-Wilson, had a miraculous escape, being thrown clear of the plane when it crashed. Immelmann landed at the site and chatted with the wounded observer and later visited him in hospital.

Immelmann expended about 400 rounds in bringing down this B.E.2c No. 2003 of No. 16 Squadron, RFC on October 10, 1915 for his fourth victory. The plane slammed into a row of trees not far from Lille and, as is evident, was a complete wreck. The pilot, 2/Lt. J. Gay, died of his wounds shortly after the event. The observer, Lt. D. Leeson, suffered only a slight leg wound and was taken prisoner. The crew had been defenceless almost from the start of the fight when a lucky shot of Immelmann's put the observer's machine gun out of action.

new assignment leaving his rival to carry on at Douai. And there Immelmann scored his fourth victory on October 10. This marvelous string of victories in a little over two months and so early on in the war was again enough to trigger further recognition from his home state. Skipping over its Merit Order, which might have been the next logical award for a native Saxon after the Albert Order, the authorities went right to its ultimate tribute. On October 13 he received the Knight's Cross of the Military St. Henry Order. Immelmann himself, in telling his family about the award in a letter home later in the month, cautioned that "you must not expect that there will be a decoration for every machine shot down," but clearly, he reveled in his growing chestful of medals.

Immelmann's fifth victory was scored on October 26 but, typically, Boelcke had already reached that level when, 10 days earlier, he had downed a French Voisin flying from his base at Rethel in the Champagne. Boelcke went one up again with a victory on October 30. The Prussians decided this called for something special and promptly, on November 1, Boelcke was in receipt of a telegram from the Chief of the German General Staff, Erich von Falkenhayn, saying that the *Kaiser* had been pleased to award him the Knight's Cross with Swords of the Royal Hohenzollern House Order in view of his magnificent achievements against enemy airmen. It was quite an honor at the time and Boelcke was the first airman to have received it.[16] But in their see-saw battle for top scoring honors in the air service Immelmann once again drew even. On November 7 he brought down another B.E.2c, this time from No. 10 Squadron, RFC, mortally wounding both the pilot and the observer. A day or two later Immelmann received an almost identical telegram from von Falkenhayn informing him that he, too, was being awarded the Hohenzollern. There was only one other Saxon officer who held the Knight's Cross with Swords at that point in the war so Immelmann had a right to be pleased. The Prussians believed in a strict progression from lower awards to higher ones and now that each of the two men had the

Hohenzollern, the only thing that remained was the coveted *Orden Pour le Mérite*. One must wonder if they thought it within reach and what it might take to earn it inasmuch as only three junior officers had so far received it in the war.[17]

Immelmann's next honor was not one that he could wear although he professed to be as pleased with it as with another order or decoration. He had attended a banquet on the evening of November 14 which included such notables as the King of Saxony, Friedrich August III, Crown Prince Rupprecht of Bavaria and Prince Ernst Heinrich, Duke of Saxony. The next day the Saxon king was scheduled to inspect *Feldflieger-Abteilung 24* and Immelmann was ordered to fly over to its field and put on a demonstration with his *Eindecker*. At the conclusion of his exhibition and after much photo taking, including some snaps made by the king himself, Friedrich August presented Immelmann with a porcelain plate from the royal factory at Meissen that His Majesty had personally selected. It portrayed a German *Taube* ("Dove" - an early unarmed monoplane) in combat with an enemy biplane.

After a bit of leave, Immelmann was back at the front again in December and was reunited with Boelcke when the latter returned to *Feldflieger-Abteilung 62* on December 11. They were still dead even in the victory column with six each and a spell of bad weather lasting through the month dimmed prospects for either of them to increase their scores. Nonetheless, it was Immelmann who triumphed that month and for once surged ahead of Boelcke in their race.

On December 15 he shot down a Morane Parasol near Valenciennes. By the time he could get up to Valenciennes where the wreckage had been taken so that he could once again be photographed with one of his victims, the bodies of the two young Englishmen had been removed. Three days later he again dined with the Bavarian Crown Prince and a small number of his retinue. Immelmann must have made a good impression at their earlier

---

[16] No awards of the Knight's Cross with Swords of the Royal Hohenzollern House Order were made in 1914 and only 59 in all were bestowed in 1915, with most of these going to staff officers. It began to be more widely awarded in the fall of 1916. A total of 748 were given that year. Distribution was much more liberal in 1917 and 1918 when 7,484 more crosses were awarded.

[17] The first award of a *Pour le Mérite* in the war went to a mere *Leutnant* who bluffed the Belgian Fort Malonne to capitulate to him and his handful of troops on August 24, 1914. The other two had gone to especially successful submarine commanders, one in 1914 and one the next year.

A photographer was conveniently on hand when Immelmann landed next to his fifth victory which he downed on October 26, 1915. Its upper wing is just visible here.

As he removes his flight clothes, we can see that even in combat Immelmann was proudly wearing his newly awarded Knight's Cross of the Military St. Henry Order.

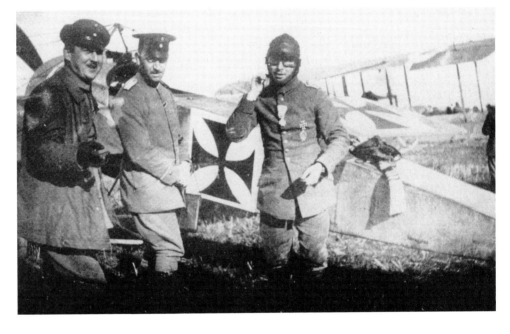

Guards are mounted next to Vickers F.B. 5 "Gunbus" No. 5462 of No. 11 Squadron, RFC to prevent souveniring. The plane was brought down near Ecoust St. Mein and the crew, Capt. C.C. Darley, pilot, and 2/Lt. R.J. Slade, observer, were made P.O.W.

On November 15, 1915 Immelmann put on a display of flying for King Friedrich August III of Saxony when His Highness visited *Feldflieger-Abteilung 24*. Afterwards, the king presented Immelmann with a Meissen plate which he is holding here. The badge at his neck is supposed to be the *Pour le Mérite*. It was touched in here since he would not earn it until two months later. The king is on Immelmann's left (with bowed head) and on his right is *Hauptmann* Meinhard Rosenmüller, the Commanding Officer of *FFl.Abt. 24*. Rosenmüller had received the Knight's Cross of the Military St. Henry Order on September 4, 1915.

The wreckage of Immelmann's seventh victory had already been carted back to Valenciennes from its crash site northeast of the city by the time he could be photographed with it. The date was December 15, 1915 and the enemy plane, which had nose-dived into the ground under Immelmann's fire, was Morane Parasol Type LA No. 5087 from No. 3 Squadron, RFC. The pilot, 2/Lt. A.V. Hobbs, and the observer, 2/Lt. C.E.G. Tudor-Jones, were both killed. Immelmann thought that Tudor-Jones had suffered a jammed machine gun and could not continue to defend themselves.

2/Lt. A. V. Hobbs, pilot of the Morane Parasol that became Immelmann's seventh victory, here in the uniform of the Royal West Sussex Regiment, his unit before being seconded to the Royal Flying Corps.

2/Lt. C. E. G. Tudor-Jones, East Lancashire Regiment and Royal Flying Corps, the observer who along with Hobbs was shot down and killed by Immelmann on December 15, 1915.

The Great War trio of medals belonging to Tudor-Jones consisting of the 1914-15 Star, the 1914-1920 War Medal and the World War I Victory Medal, affectionately known as "Pip, Squeak and Wilfred." Even though Tudor-Jones did not survive to receive these medals, they were presented to immediate survivors, named to the recipient.

Widows or parents of World War I British casualties were also presented with bronze memorial plaques inscribed with the man's name. Note here a mistake seems to have been made in that an additional "Tudor" has been inserted between his first two Christian names and his last name.

encounter the previous month for as they were about to sit down, Rupprecht invested him with his Military Merit Order, 4th Class with Swords. On Christmas Day 1915 both he and Boelcke were presented with what well may have been the first awards of the then-new *Ehrenbecher*, or Honor Goblet, a cup that was meant to signify a man's first victory.[18] So with seven victories and seven awards for bravery plus his *Ehrenbecher* Immelmann closed out 1915 and entered the final year of his short life.

Boelcke evened the contest again by scoring on January 5. The same day he also teamed up with another *Eindecker* exponent of *Feldflieger-Abteilung 62*, *Leutnant* Ernst Hess, and the pair forced another British machine down.[19] Magnanimously, Boelcke allowed full credit to go to Hess although it must have been tempting to claim a "double" and go one up again on Immelmann. Then, for the first time, Boelcke and Immelmann scored on the same day, January 12, but in widely separated actions. Boelcke's victory was a lone affair with his quarry falling into the little village of Mouscron just over the Belgian border north of Douai between the cities of Lille and Courtrai. Immelmann was patrolling well to the south in the Arras-Bapaume area with *Leutnant* Albert Osterreicher, also in an *Eindecker*. Shell bursts by German flak directed them to their target which turned out to be a Vickers F.B.5 "pusher."[20] Immelmann overtook the enemy plane first. As he closed, the British machine turned and retreated west, but coming head-on at Immelmann in the process. The observer opened fire but Immelmann sped by unscathed and turned to get on the tail of the Vickers. The Englishman also turned and in this fashion they circled in what was called "the dance of death." Both fired when the opportunity presented itself but a second burst of 100 rounds by Immelmann set the enemy on fire and it went down trailing smoke. The observer was dead or dying but the pilot was only lightly wounded and

despite the flames which ordinarily would have doomed both men, he got down to a smooth landing. Once again, the eager Immelmann set down himself, this time in a field about a half mile away, and reached the scene where he had a pleasant chat with the survivor who knew him by reputation.

The two victorious German airmen made their separate ways back to Douai where champagne was waiting at a late supper to celebrate the latest successes of the valorous pair. Just as they were sitting down, Boelcke was called to the telephone. When he heard the message, he thought it was a prank of some sort but then convinced that what he heard was legitimate, he called Kastner to the phone and returned to his seat saying nothing. Kastner returned and began the customary little speech of congratulations that marked occasions like this. Immelmann was not paying very close attention to the words of praise (which he had certainly heard before). But when Kastner began talking about this day being a milestone in German aviation and a turning point for the air service so far as recognition from the highest authorities was concerned, Immelmann perked up. Then the words came out. As a reward for the continued accomplishments of the two men, the Emperor was graciously pleased to bestow on them his highest war order, the *Pour le Mérite*. Immelmann and Boelcke were overwhelmed by the news, hardly daring to expect such a high honor so soon on the heels of the Hohenzollerns that each had received just two months earlier. In the days that followed they were showered with congratulations, feted by royalty and high ranking officers and they became instant overnight heroes throughout Germany. With these, the first air awards of the *Pour le Mérite* coming as they did after eight confirmed victories, a precedent was set. There would be 10 more awards of the "Blue Max" to fighter pilots on the Western Front before 1916 was over and in each of these instances, the

---

[18] The *Ehrenbecher* was a heavy silver (later steel) drinking mug embossed with the inscription *Dem Sieger im Luftkampfe* ("To the Victor in Air Battle") and showing in relief two eagles locked in combat with one getting the upper hand. Obviously not a wearable award, it was nonetheless considered an official one and as such was entered in on a man's service record. The initial funds had been provided by "Friends of Aviation," presumably aircraft manufacturers but it was also said the *Kaiser* and the German Crown Prince were among the donors. There are statements that by 1918 it

took multiple victories, perhaps as many as five, to earn the award but no official documentation to this effect has as yet been found. Just as they shared a victory, two-seater crews each received an *Ehrenbecher* for a successful combat.

[19] Hess went on to become an eventual 17-victory ace and was killed in action on December 23, 1917 while serving as the leader of *Jagdstaffel 19*.

[20] So-named because the engine was mounted in the rear behind the two man crew.

Victory No. 8 was an important one for Immelmann. It resulted in the award of the coveted *Orden Pour le Mérite* on the very evening of the event, January 12, 1916. Boelcke had also scored his eighth that day and he and Immelmann became the first aviation recipients of the order. Here is what was left of Immelmann's victim, Vickers F.B.5 No. 5460 of No. 11 Squadron, RFC, crewed by pilot 2/Lt. H. T. Kent and observer 2/Lt. S. Hathaway. Hathaway was killed instantly in the fight and Kent wounded slightly by a bullet that ricocheted off the engine.

Victory No. 9, a Morane-Saulnier B.B. No. 5137 of No. 3 Squadron, RFC brought down by Immelmann on March 2, 1916, became the subject of a postcard by the Berlin photographer, W. Sanke. Note the caption misidentifies it as a French airplane. Again, Immelmann put the observer out of action, killing him with many well placed shots. He was Lt. H. F. Birdwood. The pilot, 2/Lt. C. W. Palmer, was wounded in the foot and captured. His leg was later amputated and he died of blood poisoning on March 29. Immelmann said the Morane had machine guns for both pilot and observer.

recipient had scored at least eight victories before the award was approved.[21]

Boelcke inched ahead of Immelmann again when he scored a difficult victory on January 14. He called it the hardest fight thus far in his career. He was now flying an *Eindecker* with two guns but took several hits, including a shot that went through the sleeve of his clothing. Then Boelcke was again transferred out of *Feldflieger-Abteilung 62* on January 21 to take charge of an all-fighter detachment being assembled for the massive assault on Verdun, von Falkenhayn's desperate gamble to "bleed the French army white" by drawing it into a battle of attrition at a location which, because of national pride (that term again), France would have to defend at any cost. And so the direct head-to-head competition between the two men ended as Immelmann remained behind at Douai. We shall leave Boelcke's story at this point but for reader's not familiar with the rest of it, just a few facts should suffice. On the Verdun Front Boelcke had increased his score to 18 when Immelmann was killed. The country did not feel it could afford the loss of both air heroes and Boelcke was grounded on the direct orders of the *Kaiser* himself. On option offered Boelcke was a tour of the Eastern Theater of Operations which he undertook. But events in the west forced his return. The Battle of the Somme was raging and Germany had lost control of the air there due to improved British and French aircraft and superior numbers. Boelcke was to command one of the new all-fighter units equipped with biplanes of the D-Type then coming off the German production lines. Taking charge of *Jagdstaffel 2* which included such eager young tyro pilots as Manfred von Richthofen, and equipped with superior aircraft like the superb twin-gunned Albatros D. II, he had led his unit to 51 confirmed victories by October 28, 1916, 21 of which belonged to him since taking over, making his total overall a phenomenal 40 (he had scored

one victory just before his enforced leave and after the death of Immelmann). On that day, October 28, in a close combat with British D.H.2 fighters one of his men's planes brushed his wing. The collision was slight but fatal to Boelcke. He died in the crash of his crippled aircraft. By Imperial Decree *Jasta 2* was renamed *Jasta Boelcke* on December 17, 1916.

Back at Douai, after the fuss of his *Pour le Mérite* had died down a bit, the rest of January 1916 and all of February was a quiet time for Immelmann, He lamented that not one single British plane had been seen in his patrolling area since February 5 except for one day. And on that day his aircraft was having its engine repaired and he was not up in the air. His next opportunity to score came on March 2 when he caught two of the enemy between his airfield and Valenciennes. While he got one of them down, he had to let the other go due partly to a gun jam and the fact that he found himself at a height disadvantage. Possibly this lost chance to score two victories in one day, something he claimed he had been aspiring to do ever since he became a fighter pilot, increased his determination for the encounter he had on March 13. At noon that day he was in company with still another Fokker pilot of his unit, a handsome slim Bavarian *Leutnant* by the name of Max Mulzer. Their friendship was just forming but so close did it become in the next few months, and with Mulzer's fame beginning to grow too, that one became known as "the Bavarian Max" and the other as "the Saxon Max."[22] On this sortie they jumped on an enemy plane. Both fliers fired but Immelmann's shots were the decisive ones and he took the victory. Then late that afternoon more enemy planes were reported in the area. Immelmann was up again and was able to pick off one of four he encountered in his familiar hunting ground between Douai and Arras. He had his "double."

---

[21] The third aviation *Pour le Mérite* was earned not on the Western Front but rather in the Dardanelles. The recipient was *Oberleutnant* Hans-Joachim Buddecke who was attached to the German Military Mission to Turkey and who earned the award on April 14, 1916. Records are conflicting and he might have had a few as seven victories rather than eight at the time of his award. If so, it would have been just as well deserved considering the difficulties of flying there versus the Western Front (where he had scored his first three victories) and the more limited opportunities of scoring.

[22] At Immelmann's funeral in the field, Mulzer had the honor of carrying the *Ordenskissen*, the cushion on which a

military man's decorations were displayed. Mulzer's first aerial victory came on March 30, 1916 and on July 8 he shot down his eighth enemy plane and received the *Orden Pour le Mérite* that day. He was the fifth aviation recipient of the award. On September 6, with a score now standing at 10, he received the Knight's Cross of the Bavarian Military Max-Joseph Order which conferred personal nobility. He was only the second airman (out of an eventual total of 11) to receive it at that time. He thus became Max *Ritter* von Mulzer. On September 26, 1916 he was killed when the new Albatros D.I he was testing went into a side-slip and crashed.

This B.E.2c No. 4197 of No. 8 Squadron, RFC was the second of two victories scored by Immelmann on March 13, 1916, his first "double" and a feat he would perform only once again, on the day he met his own death in action. Immelmann was alone when he intercepted a flight of four of the enemy that afternoon over Arras. He fired some 500 rounds at this one which went over on its right wing and fell between Feuchy and Fampoux, turning over three times as it did. It became his 11th confirmed victory. His 10th was Bristol Scout No. 4678 of No. 4 Squadron, RFC.

The unfortunate crew of Immelmann's 11th victory, Lt. G. D. Grune, pilot, and 2/Lt. B. E. Glover, observer. Their bodies had already been moved from the crash scene by the time Immelmann got there for his customary photograph of the remains of his latest victory. However, it was too dark and he was never recorded with it.

A day or two after this event, Immelmann was detailed to patrol the skies over the spot where the Mayor of Hamburg was inspecting regiments containing men from his city. Nothing untoward happened and the Mayor was in no danger but for his services that day, Immelmann received the Hamburg Hanseatic Cross on March 15.[23] The double victory had brought his score to 11 and now with the prospects of number 12 in the offing, talk began going around that there might be something special awaiting him to mark the occasion. The king may well have initiated the idea and the unofficial word was that he had a "surprise" in store for Immelmann when the event occurred. So far, his major awards had all been linked to his moving up the scoring ladder in neat steps - at four he had received the Military St. Henry Order, at six the Hohenzollern, at eight the *Pour le Mérite,* so why not something for 12? Immelmann openly wondered what it would be. There weren't many options. For a man of his rank, he already possessed the highest awards his own Saxony and Prussia could bestow. At any rate, he would not have long to wait before he found out.

On March 29 Immelmann came across a flight of five F.E.2bs of No. 23 Squadron, RFC. It was a type yet to appear on his victory list and formidable for its day. Another "pusher," its observer seated just ahead of the pilot could fire in a wide field to the front and also protect the rear of the plane by firing back over the top wing although to do so required him to unstrap himself and stand with only his legs bracing himself, a precarious perch to say the least. He forced one of the five "Fees" down in German lines where the crew, with pilot wounded, were taken prisoner. Immelmann almost got another one of the flight but then found all his ammunition gone and there was no choice but to quit the combat and return to his field. But number 12 was safely in the bag and now the waiting for the "surprise" began. Nothing happened that evening. The next day was business as usual and Immelmann chalked up his 13th, still another unfortunate B.E.2c. No calls, no messages

came that evening either. The suspense was broken the following day, March 31. First there was a letter from the *Kaiser* which might have been something of a let-down because it was merely a congratulatory message. It expressed Wilhelm's appreciation for Immelmann's achievements in the air and was practically a carbon copy of one Boelcke had received from the Emperor on March 21 when he had scored his own 12th victory (again, a step ahead of Immelmann). In Immelmann's case, his letter had to be altered to catch up with events. When it was typed it contained the number 12 but before it could be posted, Immelmann had scored again so the word *"zwölftes"* was crossed out and *"dreizehnte"* written in by hand to make it current. It also contained one line that sounded rather petulant. The *Kaiser* reminded Immelmann that "not long ago I showed you the importance I attach to your valiant deeds by conferring on you the *Orden Pour le Mérite,* my highest war order." Was this simply a way to let Immelmann know that so far as Prussia was concerned, he could expect no further awards? Or had the Prussians found out that Immelmann was in for some further Saxon honor to mark his 12th victory and the *Kaiser* wanted to emphasize the fact that, so far as he was concerned, Immelmann had already received the highest recognition possible?

At any rate, a second communication followed the *Kaiser's* letter the same day. Crown Prince Georg of Saxony informed Immelmann that he was being awarded the Commander's Cross, 2nd Class of the Military St. Henry Order. The king had indeed delivered a real surprise. For a man of his rank it was an unprecedented honor. And for a flier, an order in that grade was a near-unique one in the war as has already been mentioned.[24] Immelmann left no doubt about how he viewed this latest recognition. He wrote that to him, a Saxon, it was a higher order than the *Pour le Mérite.* That sentiment would certainly have been shared in Dresden. The reaction in Berlin might have been a bit different to say the least.

[23] While the old Hanseatic League had been dissolved in 1669, the name had stuck and the city was known as the Free- and Hansa City of Hamburg. Its sister cities of Bremen and Lübeck also awarded their own Hanseatic Crosses, identical to Hamburg's except for different center medallions and combinations of red and white on the ribbons, these being the colors of the League.

[24] *Prinz* Friedrich Sigismund of Prussia, who earned the St.

Henry Knight's Cross in *Feldflieger-Abteilung 22,* was, like all princes of the royal house, invested with Prussia's highest orders upon reaching age 10. These included the Grand Commander of the Royal Hohenzollern House Order. Swords were added to the insignia in the war but this was in recognition of his station rather than his bravery. It cannot be considered on a par with Immelmann's award as a result.

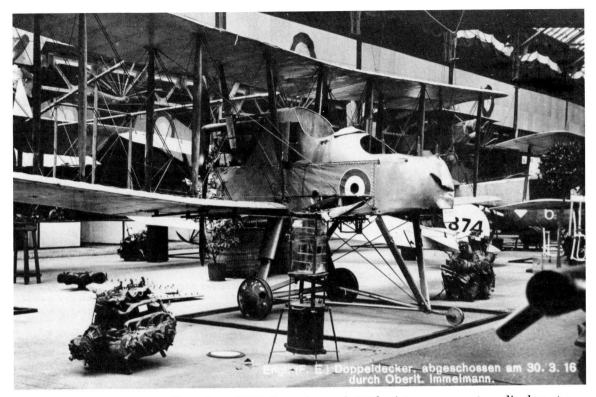

F.E.2b No. 6352 of No. 23 Squadron, RFC, Immelmann's 12th victory, was put on display at a Delka exhibition in Berlin. The last three numbers "352" are visible on the rudder. However, the date on the caption is incorrect. Immelmann shot this plane down on March 29, 1916, not March 30. It landed in German lines at Bethincourt with a wounded pilot, 2/Lt. F. G. Pinder, and an unwounded observer, 2/Lt. F. A. Halford.

The plane Immelmann shot down on March 30, 1916 for his 13th victory was this B.E.2c No. 4116 of No. 15 Squadron, RFC. It had been on a photographic mission when Immelmann caught it, killing the pilot, 2/Lt. G.J.L. Welsford. The observer, Lt. Wayland-Joyce, landed the aircraft near Alblainzeville and was captured. This was an important victory for Immelmann as it brought him even again with Boelcke for top scoring honors among pilots in the German Army Air Service.

All this while the idea of a permanent military career was growing on Immelmann as well it might with all that was coming his way. When he mentioned that he was thinking of applying for reinstatement on the active list, the Saxon Crown Prince offered nothing but encouragement. The king was quick to bless the idea and felt a promotion in grade was also indicated. Thus on April 18 he became an *Oberleutnant* in the Royal Saxon Army as an Active, or Regular, Officer.

April and May, however, were slow months for Immelmann in the scoring column. He had only one success each month. He complained that the English fliers seldom came over during this time. The April victory occurred on the 23rd in company with Mulzer again. They sighted a Vickers F.B.5 of No. 11 Squadron, RFC and Mulzer attacked first, followed by Immelmann. And once again it was Immelmann who received the credit. On that date the Royal Flying Corps Communique noted:

"2 Lt W.C.M. Phelan and 2 Lt W.A. Scott-Brown started on photographic duty at 8:45 a.m. Their machine was brought down as the result of a fight in the air, and the pilot and observer were taken prisoner."

The May success came on the 16th. Immelmann came up behind a single-seater Bristol Scout whose pilot was intent on firing at two L.V.G.s of *Feldflieger-Abteilung 62.* Immelmann dove on the unsuspecting Englishman with his twin-gunned *Eindecker* and put an economic burst squarely into it with what he was sure was telling effect. The enemy plane heeled over and went into a spin. Ground haze prevented Immelmann from observing the final outcome but upon his return he found the crew of one of the two-seaters claiming the victory since the wreckage had already been found within German lines. The matter was settled in Immelmann's favor when an examination of the body of the British pilot showed that he had been killed by a shot coming from above and behind which could only have come from his guns. The RFC Communique for May 16 carried this terse and laconic entry:

"2 Lt Mowatt, 11 Sqn, left his aerodome at 4:55 p.m. in a Bristol Scout. He has not returned."

In the letter home that described this, his 15th victory, Immelmann mentioned that he had just received two decorations from Germany's ally, Turkey. These were its Imtiaz Medal in Silver with Clasp and Sabers which automatically carried with it the award of its War Medal.[25] These were his last awards save one. His final honor was the Friedrich Cross, 2nd Class from the Duchy of Anhalt. The date of the award has not been determined nor does Immelmann refer to it in any of his correspondence. It came too late for him ever to be photographed wearing it but it took its place on the *Ordenskissen* carried at his funeral.[26]

On May 31 Immelmann had his nearest brush with death yet and as it turned out, it was an ominous harbinger of things to come. He was on the prowl again with Mulzer and, this time, with a novice, *Unteroffizier* Wolfgang Heinemann. German anti-aircraft fire directed the trio to a flight of seven "Vickers." They were, in fact, five F.E.2bs and two Martinsydes. Immelmann picked out one which went into a steep glide under his attack. He let this one go as Mulzer was also after it and turned his attention to the others, two of which were about to pounce on Heinemann. As Immelmann opened fire to spook them off Heinemann's tail, a tremendous jolt shook his Fokker E.IV. He immediately cut the ignition and began wrestling with the controls as the plane, shuddering and shaking, fell. The engine bed had broken loose throwing the motor too far forward. The machine was entirely out of balance. But with all the oscillations the motor was thrown back into position and the center of gravity had more or less been restored. By pulling back on the stick gingerly, Immelmann was able to right the fall and got down safely. The problem became apparent upon examination. A failure in the interrupter gear had caused one of his guns to sever a propeller blade. This had produced the severe tremors that had nearly shaken the aircraft apart. The only good news of the day was that Mulzer

[25] The Turkish War Medal was a red-enamelled pin-back badge in the shape of a five-pointed star with a silver half-moon crescent in the center. The Germans dubbed it the *Eiserner Halbmond* (the Iron Half-Moon or Crescent Moon) while the British referred to it as the Gallipoli Star.

[26] This award may have come as a result of Immelmann's

close connections with Boelcke. Boelcke's family had moved to Dessau in Anhalt when he was a child and was considered a native of that duchy (and not a Saxon). Boelcke also had its Friedrich Cross but in addition, both grades of the Knight's Cross with Swords of its House Order of Albert the Bear.

Zu Meiner Freude erfahre Jch, daß Sie wiederum ein feindliches Flug-
zeug -Jhr zweites- außer Gefecht gesetzt haben.Jch spreche Jhnen aus
dieser Veranlassung gern von Neuem Meine vollste Anerkennung für Jhre
vortrefflichen Leistungen im Luftkampf aus, wie Jch Jhnen schon kürz-
lich durch Verleihung des Ordens pour le mérite,Meines höchsten Kriegs-
ordens,gezeigt habe,welchen Wert Jch Jhrer kühnen Tatigkeit beimesse.-
Großes Hauptquartier,den 30.März 1916.

An den Königlich Sächsischen Leutnant der Reserve Jmmelmann bei der
Feldflieger-Abteilung 62.

The letter *Kaiser* Wilhelm II sent to Immelmann on March 30, 1916 congratulating him on his 13th victory and reminding him he had already recognized him with his highest war order, the *Pour le Mérite* (see text for details).

This photograph of Immelmann with a high ranking officer, possibly royalty, shows off his Turkish War Medal to good advantage. It is the star-shaped badge between his Iron Cross, 1st Class and long ribbon bar.

In what was probably a party for officers of air units in the Douai area, Immelmann is obviously the center of attention. The deeply tanned faces and white foreheads suggest this photograph was taken in early summer shortly before his death. The arm patch on the man seated third from the right reads "201" standing for *Artillerie-Flieger-Abteilung 201* which was located at La Brayelle near Douai in June 1916.

had gotten his man and that Heinemann had gotten down without further incident.

In this case we can turn to a very extensive report of the day's action in the RFC Communique of May 31 to get the British point of view of what occurred. Practically the entire report was devoted to the combat, which read in full:

"A fine day but thick haze made observation difficult, and little artillery work was completed.

The IIIrd Army reconnaissance, consisting of five F.E.2bs and two Martinsydes, was attacked by three Fokkers when over the locality of Cambrai. The enemy were first seen diving at our machines from the rear, with the sun at their backs. Our machines, which were heavily fired at, retaliated as occasion offered, by either firing over the top of the planes to the rear or else by partially turning and bringing the front gun into play. 2 Lt Powell, observer, in one of our F.E.'s was shot through the head and instantly killed whilst firing his gun. The machine was safely brought back and landed at its aerodome. Soon after the fight began one of the Fokkers was seen to turn half a loop, side-slip badly and nose-dive. It was last seen nose diving having apparently been hit by fire from an F.E. Another of our F.E.'s, pilot 2 Lt Cairnduff, observer Cpl Maxwell, was last seen soon after the commencement of the fight. Owing to the fact that all the machines were busily engaged in the running fight which was of a persistent nature, the fate of this machine was not observed. About the same time however, 2 Lt Watson, pilot of one of our F.E.'s reports that an F.E. apparently out of control, dived over him, almost touching his top plane. No more was seen of this machine. The two remaining Fokkers pursued our reconnaissance, one breaking off the fight or else being compelled to descend before reaching the lines, while the third one followed until within the zone of the advanced German A.A. guns. Several of our machines were badly hit in this encounter. The reconnaissance formation appears to have been kept very well until after our lines were reached.

Except for the above, very few hostile aircraft were seen, and there was only one other indecisive combat."

It was now decided that the two-seaters of *Feldflieger-Abteilung 62* would be transferred to the Eastern Front and this despite the fact that the long planned British offensive along the Somme, to be known by that name, was in its build-up stages. Since there was little aerial opposition in Russia, the Fokkers and their fighter pilots would remain behind. On June 12 they were formally detached and designated *Kampfeinsitzer-Kommando III* or, alternately, *Kampfeinsitzer-Kommando Douai (KEK III* and *KEK Douai)*. The two-seater men said their goodbyes on June 15 and in their place a Bavarian section, *Feldflieger-Abteilung 5b,* moved onto the airfield.

June 18 was the last day in the life of Max Immelmann. The weather cleared by noon but no enemy planes were reported until late in the afternoon. From then until last light on that summer evening there was much aerial activity on both sides. At about 5:00 p.m. Immelmann attacked F.E.2b 6940 of No. 25 Squadron, RFC in his Fokker E.IV 127/16 armed with two guns. The enemy plane came down in German lines with the pilot dead and the observer wounded. Back in the unit's mess after landing with his somewhat battle damaged E.IV, Immelmann got the word that another enemy formation was crossing the lines. Heinemann and he responded, the other pilots of *KEK Douai* already being up on a late patrol. Immelmann had to settle for an older 100 h.p. Fokker E.III, 246/16, which was on reserve since the E.IV still needed work. Heinemann was off just ahead of him and together they found four other Fokkers already engaged with four Englishmen. Farther on, two more Fokkers were mixing it up with four other of the enemy. Another two *Eindeckers* were jockeying into position to go after three more of the intruders. By the standards of the day, it was a huge air battle.

As he moved in for his attack, Immelmann had to fire a white signal flare in order to get the German anti-aircraft batteries, which were still banging away at the British plans, to cease. It was at 9:45 p.m. German Time, one hour ahead of British Summer Time, when his shots mortally wounded one of the F.E. pilots and the aircraft came down in German lines with its observer also wounded, but less seriously so. So Immelmann had his 16th and 17th victories, another "double." There were still many targets around and the

Two views of Immelmann's 17th and last victory scored on June 18, 1916 in the late evening hours shortly before he himself was killed in action. The photographs were obviously taken in daylight, probably the following morning. In the one at the top, F.E.2b No. 6940 of No. 25 Squadron, RFC is in the process of being salved. The 17-year old pilot, 2/Lt. J.R.B. Savage, died of his wounds. The observer was also wounded but survived as a prisoner. He was a non-commissioned officer, 2nd Air Mechanic P. Robinson. In the photo below a pensive group of German officers, including Immelmann's close friend, Max Mulzer, third from the right, inspect No. 6940, dubbed "Baby Mine," now stripped of its armament and minus its undercarriage.

Three views of the jumble of wires, tubing and smashed parts of Immelmann's Fokker E. III 246/16, one on the crash site itself and two in a shed where the wreckage was taken for evaluation and determination of what caused the fatal crash. In the photograph below note the severed arm of the one remaining blade of the propeller and the nearly intact aft section of the fuselage and rudder. The generally accepted view was that Immelmann had shot off a blade due to faulty synchronization and the resultant vibrations caused the plane to break up.

Lt. G. R. McCubbin, pilot of the F.E.2b of No. 25 Squadron, RFC who, along with his observer, was credited with shooting Immelmann down. He received the Distinguished Service Order for the feat and is shown here wearing its ribbon under his wings.

Corp. J. H. Waller (here a Sergeant), McCubbin's observer, was the gunner whose fire the British claimed caused Immelmann's *Eindecker* to break up. For his part in the action he was decorated with the Distinguished Conduct Medal.

Waller's original medals mounted "Court Style." From left to right they are: The Distinguished Conduct Medal, the Military Medal (which he had received before the Immelmann action for his generally good work), the 1914-1920 War Medal, the World War I Victory Medal and the Russian Medal of St. George, 1st Class. The Russian award also came for downing Immelmann and, properly, there should be a bow on the ribbon to denote it was in the 1st Class, not the 2nd Class, both being in gold. The 3rd Class was in silver with bow and the 4th just plain silver.

Squadron: 25

Type and No. of aeroplane: F.E.2b.6346

Armament: 2 Lewis Guns

Pilot: 2/Lt.G.R.McCubbin

Observer: Corpl.J.H.Waller

Locality: ANNAY

Date: 18th June,1916.

Time: 9.5 p.m.

Duty: Patrol

Height: 9,000 ft.

Immelman

Remarks on Hostile machine:-Type, armament, speed, etc.

2 FOKKERS.

- Narrative -

At about 9 p.m. whilst on patrol duty over LOOS, three Fokkers were seen behind the lines. Lieut.McCubbin proceeded over the lines towards them. One Fokker diver away from the other two and left them. The remaining two made for LENS, towards another F.E. Lieut. McCubbin followed them. Whilst one of them was attacking the F.E. piloted by 2/Lt. Savage (both machines diving steeply) Lieut. McCubbin dived towards the attacking machine and fired upon it. Immediately the Fokker turned to the right from the other F.E. and dived perpendicularly towards the ground. It was seen to crash by 22 Anti Aircraft battery.

The second Fokker was either above or directly behind Lt. McCubbin's machine. After he turned he saw neither the F.E. nor the two Fokkers.

R.R. CHERRY.
Major,
Commanding No.25 Squadron,
R.F.C.

In the Field,

19th June, 1916.

CERTIFIED TRUE COPY

HA Jones 9th June, 1936.

Original extracted for permanent retention by the Squadron.

See A.M. file No.356121/34.

A "Certified True Copy" of the Combat Report under the name of the Commanding Officer of No. 25 Squadron, RFC describing Immelmann's final combat.

melee continued. Thoughts of scoring a "hat trick" had to be in his mind as he looked for another target. All the other German pilots were heavily engaged so only witnesses on the ground saw what happened as Immelmann attacked still another F.E. His Fokker began the same strange oscillations again. With bracing wires flaying, the tubing of the fuselage began to crack as the aircraft slewed around. Within seconds the rear portion was torn loose. The forward half, with the dead weight of the engine, dropped like a stone with a trapped Immelmann. The wings collapsed and separated. Motor, pilot and what was left of the fuselage smashed into the earth, killing Immelmann instantly. The first Germans reaching the crash site extricated the body and when opening the leather flight jacket, immediately knew who it was. Immelmann was wearing his *Pour le Mérite*.

The death of so great a hero obviously required that a formal inquiry into the circumstances be conducted. There were several theories that had to be investigated, including the obvious one that he might have been shot down by the F.E. he was attacking. Much more acceptable from the German side, however were these. Perhaps Immelmann's Fokker had been hit by friendly anti-aircraft fire which so weakened the structure of the aircraft that it collapsed in the violent maneuvering that ensued. Or perhaps there had been a malfunction again and he had shot off part of his propeller and this caused the fatal vibrations that had wrenched the plane apart. Anything would have been preferable to the idea that Immelmann had been vanquished in the air. The inquiry never reached a definite conclusion but the prevailing German opinion was that he had shot off his own propeller. For example, Boelcke wrote:

"Immelmann lost his life by a silly chance. All that is written in the papers about a fight in the air, etc., is rot. A bit of his propeller flew off; the jarring tore the bracing wires connecting up with the fuselage, and then that broke away."

In a post-war account of Immelmann's last combat written by a Rudolf Heinemann that appeared in the *Berliner Nachtausgabe* (Berlin Evening Extra), he claimed to have examined the wreckage after the remains had been moved to a shed. He stated that one of the blades had been practically sawed off. The stump was in direct line with the path of bullets that would have come from Immelmann's gun according to this account.[27]

Understandably, the British preferred to believe that Immelmann had been shot down by the Royal Flying Corps. In the official Communique they made no definite claim at the time but, later, the No. 25 Squadron crew of 2/Lt. G. R. McCubbin and Corp. J. H. Waller were given credit for the victory and decorated for their feat. The British view of the combat in the Communique read:

"An F.E. of 25 Sqn, pilot 2 Lt McCubbin, observer, Cpl Waller, when patrolling over Annay at about 9:00 p.m. attacked three Fokkers seen behind the lines.[28] One of the latter went off. The remaining two made for Lens towards another F.E. of 25 Sqn, pilot, 2 Lt Savage, observer, AM Robinson, which they attacked.[29]

Lt McCubbin followed and joined the fight, diving on to one of the attacking Fokkers which turned away and dived perpendicularly towards the ground. It was seen to crash by the 22nd A.A. battery. When Lt McCubbin turned again the other F.E. and Fokker had disappeared. The second F.E., 2 Lt Savage, is missing and is reported to have landed in the enemy's lines without crashing."

Funeral ceremonies for Immelmann were held in Douai on June 22. As the accompanying photographs show, it was an elaborate and typically Teutonic affair. In attendance were Crown Prince Georg of Saxony, Crown Prince Rupprecht of Bavaria (who commanded the German 6th Army to which *KEK Douai* was attached), other high officers of the 6th Army and

---

[27] This Rudolf Heinemann also said in the article that both he and his brother, Wolfgang, were up in the air with Immelmann that day. All known accounts mention only the presence of Wolfgang however.

[28] 9:00 p.m. British Summer Time would be 10:00 p.m. German Time on this date.

[29] "AM" was an abbreviation for the enlisted rank of Air

Mechanic. The observer gunners in the F.E. squadrons (and others) were sometimes non-commissioned officers as were a few pilots. In conventional German two-seater units, while the pilots were not infrequently non-commissioned officers, the observers were always officers (although in the special *Schlachtstaffeln* both crew members were usually enlisted men).

The elaborate funeral ceremonies for Immelmann in Douai were typically Teutonic. Torches flared atop the four obelisks that flanked his casket as he lay in state in the courtyard of a hospital there.

A guard of honor stands at attention with fixed bayonets. A leather crash helmet has been placed on the casket at the foot of which the *Ordenskissen* displaying his awards can be seen.

The procession with Immelmann's flag draped casket on a gun carriage approaching the railway station in Douai. The many floral tributes are carried by enlisted men. Immediately behind the gun carriage the figure of Immelmann's close friend, Max Mulzer wearing his own medals, can be seen carrying the *Ordenskissen*.

A close-up view of Immelmann's *Ordenskissen*. The badge with the long neck ribbon is the Commander's Cross of the Military St. Henry Order. His Knight's Cross of that order leads off his order bar followed by his two other Saxon awards, two Prussian and then one each from Bavaria, the Hanseatic City of Hamburg and Anhalt. Above the bar is his *Pour le Mérite*. In addition to his Iron Cross, 1st Class and Pilot's Badge pinned to the cushion, we also see his two Turkish awards, the War Medal on the left and the Imtiaz Medal in Silver with Clasp and Sabers on the right.

The photograph below shows the moment when Immelmann's casket is about to be loaded on a goods wagon to take his remains for final burial ceremonies in Dresden. Mulzer with his light banded *Chevaulegers-Regiment* service cap appears at the right side of the open car door.

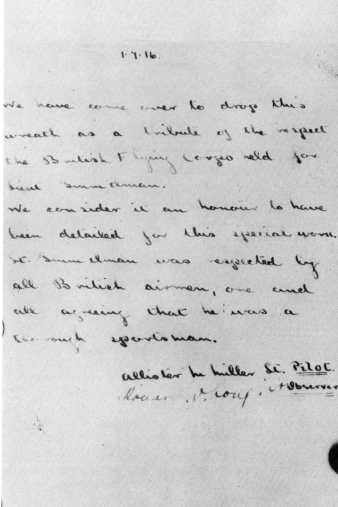

Nearly two weeks after Immelmann's death, two members of the Royal Flying Corps dropped this floral tribute to his memory. Accompanying it was a handwritten message which read:

"1.7.16
We have come over to drop this wreath
as a tribute of the respect the British
Flying Corps held for Lieut. Immelman (sic).

We consider it an honour to have been
detailed for this special work. Lt.
Immelman (sic) was respected by all British
airmen, one and all agreeing that he was a
thorough sportsman.

(signed)

Allister McMillen   Lt. Pilot
Howard O. Long   Lt. Observer"

deputations from other flying units all along the Western Front. Boelcke had received permission to fly up to Douai and he was there too. After the service which was held in the courtyard of the military hospital in Douai, Immelmann's coffin was loaded on a gun limber and a solemn procession marched to the railway station with Max Mulzer immediately behind the limber bearing the *Ordenskissen*. There the coffin was loaded aboard a goods wagon for the trip to Dresden, more ceremonies and final interment. The tributes were many but can be summed up by quoting the obituary notice signed by *Major* Friedrich Stempel, *Stabsoffizier der Flieger* of the 6th Army, which ended with these words:

"His glory and his name are his country's. In the annals of the German Flying Corps his memory will live as that of a bold flier, fighter and conqueror."

On the official list of German aces (in this case, men with four or more confirmed victories, not five as is the case on Allied lists) Immelmann's final score is always carried as 15, not the 17 he deserved. This is odd because with the incontrovertible evidence in German hands in the form of two downed aircraft with dead or wounded British airmen, what more proof was needed? Even the RFC Communiques acknowledged the two losses although, of course, they had no way of knowing who the victorious German airman was. As for the first victory on June 18, the Communique read:

"An F.E. of 25 Sqn, pilot, Lt Rogers, observer, Sgt Taylor, is missing. It was last seen west of Souchez and is reported to have landed in the enemy's lines about 3 miles north-north-east of Arras. One of the occupants was seen to get out and go into the enemy's trenches."

And for Immelmann's final victory there was this entry:

"Another machine of 25 Squadron, pilot, Lt Savage, observer, AM Robinson, is also missing, and is reported to have been shot down near Wingles in a fight with two Fokkers."

As the air war went on, Immelmann's record was eclipsed by many other German pilots.[30] Yet his 17 victories, all scored on an aircraft that in itself was never particularly outstanding, remains a remarkable achievement. That, too, could serve as a fitting epitaph for the man whose prowess in the skies over northeastern France earned him the title of *Der Adler von Lille* ("The Eagle of Lille").

The stories of the other aviation recipients of the Military St. Henry Order will have to be considerably condensed if only because of their sheer number. But even if space were no limitation, it would not be possible to write about most of their careers in the same depth as Immelmann's. For once again we encounter the old problem. The exploits of the fighter pilots, particularly their victories, were duly recorded during the war and much was written about many of them prior to World War II when documentation was readily available, access to it was easy and in many instances the men involved were still alive. Not so with most of the men who never made the transition to become a successful fighter pilot but who served exclusively in other capacities in the air war, often in near complete obscurity. Truly, they are the unsung heroes and deserve better than what they will receive here.

Fortunately, however, in the case of the aviation recipients of the Military St. Henry Order, brief citations forming the basis for their awards have been preserved. Although frequently very general in nature and with the same language used time and time again to describe a man's bravery, nerve and determination, they do provide a good idea of what it took to receive the highest recognition Saxony could bestow. These citations follow now, arranged in the chronological order of bestowal. Fully anglicized translations have been kept to a minimum so that the flavor of the original wording in German could be maintained. Where other facts are known about a particular recipient's career, these have been included.

The first aviation award of the Knight's Cross of the order was made a little more than three months into the war. It went to an observer for his consistently good work and aggressiveness, traits which, as we shall see, frequently lay behind the basis for the award. Just six days later, five more Knight's Crosses were awarded to equally

---

[30]. There are 52 German fighter pilots on the official list who were credited with 18 or more victories.

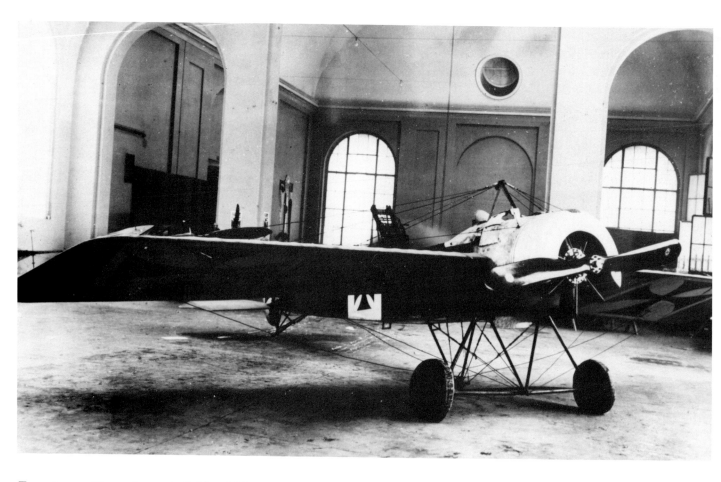

Two views of Immelmann's Fokker E.I *Eindecker,* E.3/15, which was placed on display at the Army Museum in Dresden. Its ultimate fate is unknown but it presumably did not survive World War II.

deserving pilots and observers in the early two-seaters of that time. It would turn out to be the largest number of awards of the order ever distributed within the *Fliegertruppe* in one day.

LEUTNANT EGBERT KÜHN

Awarded the Knight's Cross of the Military St. Henry Order on November 11, 1914 when serving in *Feldflieger-Abteilung 3*.

Citation: "Already a trained flier in peacetime, *Lt.* Kühn fought with his detachment in every battle, distinguishing himself through his audacity, bravery and proficiency on many flights."

Kühn was an observer and was later promoted *Oberleutnant*. On April 28, 1915, now serving with *Feldflieger-Abteilung 48,* he and his pilot, Hugo Geyer, were credited with downing a French Voisin while flying Aviatik C.68/15. Often this is recorded as the German Army Air Service's first officially confirmed victory. But there appears to be at least one other earlier claim that should be accorded this distinction.

On November 4, 1914, *Oberleutnant* Richard Flashar, later a fighter pilot and named the Commanding Officer of *Jasta 5* on June 10, 1917 and the leader of *Jagdgruppe 2* on May 12, 1918, and his observer, an *Oberleutnant* Demuth, shot down an enemy plane. It was before the day of the *Ehrenbecher* but the crew did receive a congratulatory message from the Commanding General in the 1st Army Daily Report. Then on Christmas Eve 1916, *Idflieg* presented a gold watch to him. It was inscribed with the following testimonial: *Dem Oberleutnant Flashar, Flugzeugführer des ersten, am 5 November 1914 Siegreichen deutschen Flugzeuges. Die Inspektion der Fliegertruppe* ("To Senior Lieutenant Flashar, Pilot of the First Victorious German Aircraft on 5 November 1914. The Inspectorate of Aviation"). See Appendix XV for Flashar's complete account of the action.

Not quite a month after the Kühn/Geyer victory, the crew was on another mission when their aircraft was hit by anti-aircraft fire over Dammerkirch, east of Belfort on the upper Rhine, on May 25, 1915. Kühn was mortally wounded but Geyer was unscathed and brought the plane down to a safe landing.

As mentioned in the citation, Kühn was a pre-war aviator and had been awarded the Prussian Crown Order, 4th Class without Swords (noted in the *Militär-Wochenblatt* on July 2, 1914). In peacetime, junior officers were given this award, and to a lesser extent, the Red Eagle Order, 4th Class without Swords, for meritorious service. This practice was largely discontinued during World War I. Most of the awards that were made of the Crown and Red Eagle Orders, both with and without Swords, in the 3rd and 4th Classes went to over-age-in-grade officers who were being put on the retired list. Kühn also held the Albert Order, Knight 2nd Class with Swords. On the official roll of this award the bestowal date is July 15, 1915 but an announcement of it had already appeared in the May 15, 1915 issue of *Flugsport,* a German aviation enthusiast's journal, so the date on the roll was obviously a late entry. For a native Saxon, the Albert Order would normally be awarded before the St. Henry Order (as in the case of Immelmann). The actual bestowal date of Kühn's Albert Order has not been found but it is much more likely that he received it prior to his November 11, 1914 award of the Knight's St. Henry than after it, as the *Flugsport* announcement and the date on the roll would suggest.

OBERLEUTNANT EMIL CLEMENS

Awarded the Knight's Cross of the Military St. Henry Order on November 17, 1914 when serving in *Feldflieger-Abteilung 24*.

Citation: *"Oblt.* Clemens, under orders from the 19th General Headquarters, flew a brilliant reconnaissance as a pilot on September 19, 1914 despite stormy weather. Despite difficulties and a heavy bombardment, he returned with important information. A remarkable achievement!"

Clemens was transferred to *Brieftauben-Abteilung-Ostende* on November 27, 1914 and other than he survived the war, nothing further is known of his career.

His other awards parallel those of Kühn. The *Militär-Wochenblatt* of August 15, 1914 announced his receiving the Prussian Crown Order, 4th Class without Swords. On the roll of the Albert Order he is shown as receiving the Knight 2nd Class with

Leutnant Egbert Kühn was the first aviation recipient of the Military St. Henry Order. He was awarded the Knight's Cross on November 11, 1914 but was killed in action on May 25, 1915.

A large group of German soldiers, including several other airmen, surround the wreckage of Kühn's first and only victory. On April 28, 1915 Kühn shot down this French Voisin. Kühn, with goggles on his service cap, is standing at the left with a souvenir fragment from the plane in his right hand. The tall man further to the left with his hands in his pockets and also with goggles on his cap is Hugo Geyer who was Kühn's pilot in the fight and who was also with Kühn when he was fatally hit by anti-aircraft fire.

Swords on May 3, 1915, still with *Feldflieger-Abteilung 24*. From unit records, however, we know his Albert Order was actually bestowed on October 2, 1914, thus before his St. Henry Order. Here is direct evidence that the dates on the roll can be well after the fact and must therefore be treated with that in mind.

LEUTNANT RUDOLF HASENOHR

Awarded the Knight's Cross of the Military St. Henry Order on November 17, 1914 when serving in *Feldflieger-Abteilung 24*.

Citation: "As the observer in *Oblt.* Clemens' plane *(Feldflieger-Abteilung 24),* which despite violent storms and heavy ground opposition flew courageously on September 19, 1914, *Lt.* Hasenohr, with nerves of steel, made important observations for the high command."

This was the first instance in the war of a two-seater crew being simultaneously decorated with the St. Henry Order for the same action. Hasenohr was transferred along with Clemens to *Brieftauben-Abteilung-Ostende* on November 27, 1914 and, as with Clemens, his further record in the war is unknown although he, too, survived.

Hasenohr also received the Albert Order, Knight 2nd Class with Swords in *Feldflieger-Abteilung 24* on October 2, 1914 although the date of the award as carried on the roll is, again, May 3, 1915.

OBERLEUTNANT KURT MÜLLER

Awarded the Knight's Cross of the Military St. Henry Order on November 17, 1914 when serving in *Feldflieger-Abteilung 24*.

Citation: "*Oblt.* Müller, on the orders of the 19th General Headquarters, flew a night reconnaissance mission in the autumn of 1914 and returned with extraordinarily important observations. The reconnaissance of enemy defenses and the lighted transport trains gave information on the strength and movements of the enemy. He had not been trained in flying and landing at night so this flight was an exceptionally brave deed."

Along with Clemens and Hasenohr, Müller was transferred to *Brieftauben-Abteilung-Ostende* one week after being decorated with the Knight's St. Henry. In April 1915 he was posted to *Feldflieger-Abteilung 69* on the Eastern Front. There, and now promoted *Hauptmann*, he was killed in an accident at Resiczabanga on October 15, 1915. Along with him his pilot, *Oberleutnant* Wulfgar von Koerber, also perished in the crash.

Müller was another *Feldflieger-Abteilung 24* officer to receive the Albert Order, Knight 2nd Class with Swords on October 2, 1914. The roll also shows that he was awarded the Knight 1st Class with Swords of the order in *Feldflieger-Abteilung 69*. The date is February 8, 1916 in what appears to be another late entry (although it could also have been a posthumous award since Saxony (and Bavaria) did make awards after a man's death although Prussia generally did not.)

LEUTNANT GERHARD NETTE

Awarded the Knight's Cross of the Military St. Henry Order on November 17, 1914 when serving in *Feldflieger-Abteilung 12*.

Citation: "*Lt.* Nette earned special recognition from the Army High Command for exceptionally brave achievements during the advances in the autumn of 1914."

Nette and his observer, *Oberleutnant* von Bülow-Bussow in *Feldflieger-Abteilung 12* at the time, were shot down and killed near Braisne, east of Soissons in France. A crew from *Escadrille* MS (Morane Saulnier) 12, *Adjutant Chef* Meseguich and *Sous Lieutenant* Jacottet, were credited with the victory that occurred in the early morning hours of May 26, 1915. Von Bülow-Bussow was a nephew of the later *Generalfeldmarschall* Karl von Bülow.

A *Leutnant* Gerhard Nette is carried on the roll as receiving the Albert Order, Knight 2nd Class with Swords on November 1, 1915 and Saxe-Altenburg records show a man with the same name as receiving the Knight 2nd Class with Swords of the Ernestine House Order on January 29, 1915. However, the recipient's unit is given as *Feldflieger-Abteilung 29* in both cases. It is probable that we are dealing with the same man here (with a typical late entry for the Albert Order) and a mistake was made in listing his unit. To complicate matters a bit more, *Flugsport*, in its

Leutnant Gerhard Nette in the rear pit of an Albatros B.I. Nette was awarded the Knight's Cross of the Military St. Henry Order on November 17, 1914. Pilots in the unarmed B-Type aircraft sat behind the observer. Nette's observer, shown here, was *Leutnant* Busso von Bülow.

Nette and von Bülow perished together on May 26, 1915 in combat with a French plane. The French seemed to have had a penchant for photographing cadavers. This is von Bülow's corpse. Note the upholstered seat.

The victors over Nette and von Bülow were Rene Meseguich and Paul Jacottet of M.S. 12, shown here with their Morane Parasol. Jacottet is wearing the cross of a *Chevalier* of the French Legion of Honor.

August 30, 1916 issue, mentions a *Leutnant* Nette as receiving the Saxon Merit Order, Knight 2nd Class with Swords. The St. Henry recipient, Gerhard Nette, held the Prussian Crown Order, 4th Class (without Swords) just before the war in circumstances similar to the same awards to Kühn and Clemens already mentioned.

LEUTNANT GEORG ZEUMER

Awarded the Knight's Cross of the Military St. Henry Order on November 17, 1914 when serving in *Feldflieger-Abteilung 4*.

Citation: *"Lt.* Zeumer brought back important reports from numerous flights deep in enemy territory. On one of these reconnaissance flights during the advances of the German Army in the autumn of 1914, armed only with a pistol, the brave flier attacked an English plane equipped with a machine gun and defeated it."

Presumably, this was not a decisive victory and the meaning of the term "defeated it" was that Zeumer got the better of his adversary and drove him off. In the records of the fighter unit in which he later served, no victories are listed after his name at the time of his joining it (nor would he score any during his period of service with it).

By the summer of 1915, Zeumer was flying on the Eastern Front, now assigned to *Feldflieger-Abteilung 69*. One of its fledgling observers there was the later famous Manfred von Richthofen. At the end of August, both men were transferred back to the west and sent to *Brieftauben-Abteilung-Ostende*. Zeumer and von Richthofen became a team, often flying together. In between, Zeumer also flew one of the new *Eindeckers* that were being parceled out to units like *BAO* to fly protection for its main complement which, at the time, included some of the largest twin-engined bombers then in German service.

With his single-seater experience Zeumer was in a good position to be selected to go to one of the all-fighter detachments that were being formed in August 1916 and, accordingly, he was posted to *Jasta 2* at a later date. Zeumer suffered from tuberculosis and possibly had a fatal case. A frail fellow, he was affectionately known as "the lunger." So it was perhaps merciful that he met his death in action on June 17, 1917 near La Ferrcere. He

had by then been promoted *Oberleutnant* and had passed his 27th birthday three months earlier. When von Richthofen learned of his old comrade's death, he felt it was all for the best and wrote: "Yesterday, Zeumer was killed in air combat. It was perhaps the best thing that could have happened to him. He knew that he had not much longer to live. Such an excellent and noble fellow. How he would have hated to drag himself toward the inevitable end. For him it would have been tragic. As it is, he died a heroic death before the enemy."

LEUTNANT FRIEDRICH VON HESLER

Awarded the Knight's Cross of the Military St. Henry Order on December 23, 1914 when serving in *Feldflieger-Abteilung 31*.

Citation: *"Lt.* von Hesler successfully carried out numerous reconnaissance flights against the enemy. On one flight in the east in the autumn of 1914 he was forced to land behind enemy lines near Grojec, south of Warsaw. Through prudence and outstanding bravery he returned to his own forces."

Von Hesler is listed as receiving the Albert Order, Knight 2nd Class with Swords on September 27, 1916 and the Merit Order, Knight 2nd Class with Swords with simply a "1917" date. His unit in both cases by that time was given as *Flieger-Abteilung 300*, which also carried the official designation "Pascha," and operated in Palestine. The wide spread of dates between the awards here suggests that possibly his Merit Order or both that and his Albert Order did come after his Knight's St. Henry. Von Hesler survived the war. Hereafter, unless specific mention is made of a man's death, the other St. Henry winners discussed here can also be presumed to have survived.

LEUTNANT KARL MENZEL

Awarded the Knight's Cross of the Military St. Henry Order on February 9, 1915 when serving in *Feldflieger-Abteilung 12*.

Citation: "From the end of September to early October 1914 *Lt.* Menzel distinguished himself by making three major strategic reconnaissance flights which brought back important

Leutnant Georg Zeumer (left) and an unknown companion. Zeumer received the Knight's Cross of the Military St. Henry Order on November 17, 1914 when serving as a two-seater pilot in *Feldflieger-Abteilung 4*. He died as a fighter pilot in *Jasta Boelcke* on June 17, 1917. On the lower right of his tunic he is wearing the Austro-Hungarian Field Pilot's Badge earned, no doubt, for his service on the Eastern Front in the summer of 1915.

Kampfstaffel "T", complete with musicians, holds a beer party on the Somme in the summer of 1916. The officers of the unit are seated behind the table and in four chairs to the left. *Leutnant* Friedrich von Hesler who received the Knight's Cross of the Military St. Henry Order on December 23, 1914 is the tall man seated behind the table at the left. The other man behind the table is probably the unit's Commanding Officer, *Hauptmann* Bernhardt. Seated in a chair second from the left is the later 39-victory *Pour le Mérite* ace, Heinrich Gontermann. The non-commissioned officer pilot standing with his elbow resting on von Hesler's shoulder is Hans Ruppert. Things were never this informal in the British Royal Flying Corps.

LEUTNANT KURT RÖDEL

Awarded the Knight's Cross of the Military St. Henry Order on July 18, 1915 when serving in *Feldflieger-Abteilung 58*.

Citation: *"Lt.* Rödel, after many successful missions against the enemy, showed extreme presence of mind on one particular mission. Although his aircraft was on fire in the air, he maneuvered it to a smooth landing behind his own lines."

Rödel is shown as receiving the Albert Order, Knight 2nd Class with Swords on November 18, 1915 while with *Festungs-Flieger-Abteilung 11*.

LEUTNANT KARL HANSEN

Awarded the Knight's Cross of the Military St. Henry Order on August 25, 1915 when serving in *Feldflieger-Abteilung 62*.

Citation: *"Lt.* Hansen, who has distinguished himself on many missions, forced an English plane to the ground with extreme bravery and took the two crewmen prisoner near Douai on July 29, 1915."

While the Royal Flying Corps Communique for July 29, 1915 reports a number of encounters between British and German aircraft, including brushes with aircraft identified for the first time as specifically Fokkers armed with machine guns (i.e., the Fokker E.I *Eindecker*), it makes no mention at all of any RFC losses.

RITTMEISTER PAUL DIETZE

Awarded the Knight's Cross of the Military St. Henry Order on September 4, 1915 when serving in *Feldflieger-Abteilung 24*.

Citation: "On a flight to Boulogne, *Rittm.* Dietze encountered severe storms and heavy cloudbanks. Snow showers along the coast forced him down to 2,000 meters and he became disoriented. As if that were not enough, he was bombarded with heavy anti-aircraft fire. On another mission, he engaged in an air battle and although the enemy was faster and equipped with a machine gun, he carried on the unequal fight with a carbine. He succeeded in fending off his opponent and completed his reconnaissance mission, returning through severe enemy fire. Bullet holes in the wings and a fist-sized hole in the bottom of the fuselage under the observer's seat caused by a piece of shrapnel attest to the heat of the battle."

The combat mentioned in the citation is believed to have taken place sometime in October 1914 with Dietze's observer, *Hauptmann* Meinhard Rosenmüller, manning the carbine.

Dietze received the Albert Order, Knight 2nd Class with Swords on October 2, 1914. The award was mentioned in the October 28, 1914 issue of *Flugsport*, the January 14, 1915 issue of the *Militär-Wochenblatt* and it was not until May 3, 1915 that it appears on the roll of the order, an interesting example of the discrepancy between the actual receipt of an award and when it appears in other sources. He also received the Merit Order, Knight 2nd Class with Swords on October 30, 1914 as a member of *Feldflieger-Abteilung 24*. This, however, is not mentioned in either of the two publications and the roll of awards of the Merit Order in 1914 is not available in the *Staatsarchiv* in Dresden.

LEUTNANT JOHANNES REICHEL

Awarded the Knight's Cross of the Military St. Henry Order on September 4, 1915 when serving in *Flieger-Ersatz-Abteilung I* of *Flieger-Kompagnie 13, K.u.K. Luftfahrttruppe*.

Citation: "Since November 1914, *Lt.* Reichel brought back numerous valuable flight reports in the Russian theater of operations. Especially so was the report of the unexpected appearance of a Russian corps which enabled the German troops to take measures against a surprise attack. He also reported the evacuation of a Russian corps on January 12, 1915. On an especially difficult flight in the Carpathians he was made a Russian prisoner of war only to escape six days later and hide under hard and life threatening conditions in Lemburg for four months. *Lt.* Reichel used this time to gather important military information."

Reichel was obviously serving in a German *Feldflieger-Abteilung* at the time of the events

(Above)

Rittmeister Paul Dietze, shown here (7th from the left) as the Commanding Officer of *Kampfstaffel 41* of *Kampfgeschwader 7* at Essigny le Grand in August 1916, received the Knight's Cross of the Military St. Henry Order on September 4, 1915 as a pilot in *Feldflieger-Abteilung 24*. Left to right: *Lt.* von Thomsen, *Lt.* Schmager, *Oblt.* Kuppinger, *Oblt.* Schmidt, *Lt.* von Eberstein, *Unteroffz.* Kuhn, Dietze, *Unteroffz.* Beerendonk, *Lt.* Stern, *Gefr.* Tillmanns, *Unteroffz.* Kubitza and *Gefr.* Franke. In the Fall of 1917 Dietze was the Commanding Officer of *Flieger-Abteilung (A)255*.

(Left)

Hauptmann Meinhard Rosenmüller (extreme right) was Dietze's observer in *Feldflieger-Abteilung 24* and was awarded his St. Henry Order on the same date as Dietze, September 4, 1915. Other members of the unit pictured here are, left to right: *Lt.* Grosse, *Unteroffz.* Dietrich, *Oblt.* Vogel, *Oblt.* Lerche, *Lt.* Schröter and Rosenmüller. In all, seven men in *FFl.Abt. 24* and one man in its successor unit, *Flieger-Abteilung (A)264,* received the Knight's Cross of the order, making it the most highly decorated formation for this award.

tenth victories back-to-back on September 22 and 23. These closed out his victory log in *Jasta 4*. On December 1 he was again ordered back to Turkey.

He remained in the east throughout most of 1917. His only success there came on March 30 when he was credited with two British planes downed over Smyrna, a Farman and a "Vickers." Back in the west again in time for the last big German offensive of the war, he was assigned to *Jasta 30* on February 15, 1918. But he reported there as just a regular pilot, not in the leadership position one might expect for a man of his seniority and many honors. Perhaps it was felt that before an entire *Jasta* was entrusted to him he needed some time to acclimate himself to the vastly changed conditions in the air war on the Western Front since 1916. Besides, *Jasta 30* was then in the capable hands of *Oberleutnant* Hans Bethge. He had been in charge since February 1917 and when Buddecke reported in, could boast of a victory score of 18. Buddecke got his last victory, his 13th official, on February 19 when he downed a Sopwith Camel whose wounded pilot was able to reach his own lines. Bethge also got a Camel that day.[39] Then on March 8 Buddecke was detached from *Jasta 30* and sent over to *Jasta 18*. He went there to assist its Commanding Officer, his old comrade and former subordinate, *Hauptmann* Rudolf Berthold, undoubtedly at Berthold's own request. Berthold had just reported to duty on March 1 having been out of action since the previous October when he had suffered a severe arm wound in an air combat on the 10th of the month. Buddecke was to lead *Jasta 18* in the air while Berthold retained overall command. Berthold's arm was still in a sling and

he was in no condition to fly. Just two days later, on March 10, the "Shooting Hawk" was mortally wounded and crashed to his death.[40]

In addition to the Imperial German and Turkish awards mentioned in the text, Buddecke held the Knight's Cross with Swords of the Royal Hohenzollern House Order, the Bavarian Military Merit Order, 4th Class with Swords and the Brunswick War Merit Cross, 2nd Class. He also was awarded the Austro-Hungarian Field Pilot's Badge.

OBERLEUTNANT KARL *FREIHERR* VON DEM BUSSCHE-STREITHORST

Awarded the Knight's Cross of the Military St. Henry Order on December 24, 1915 when serving in *Feldflieger-Abteilung 63*.

Citation: *"Oblt. Freiherr* von dem Bussche-Streithorst flew many missions against the enemy with the *Beskidenkorps* formation under difficult conditions and with remarkable energy. He brought back extremely important results."

Von dem Bussche-Streithorst, now prompted *Rittmeister* and flying with *Flieger-Abteilung 302* in Palestine, was killed in a crash at the El Afuleh aerodrome, about 10 miles inland from Haifa, on December 17, 1917.

HAUPTMANN ALBERT VON MALORTIE

Awarded the Knight's Cross of the Military St. Henry Order on December 24, 1915 when serving in *Feldflieger-Abteilung 63*.

---

ries during his stint with *Jasta 4*, single ones on September 11, a Nieuport, and a Caudron on October 21. The only squadron victories racked up in November all went to Bernert, three of them and, remarkably, all scored on a single day, November 9. They were tough opponents for the day, two D.H.2 single-seater fighters and an F.E.2b "pusher." Bernert was then posted to *Jasta Boelcke*. After two victories in March 1917, April saw his best string ever. He was credited with a total of 15 that month culminating with five in one day, on April 24. It was a fitting way to celebrate his *Pour le Mérite* which had been approved the day before. With effect from May 1, he was appointed to the command of *Jasta 6* and promptly added three more victories during his first week there. Injured in a crash and really a badly worn-out man, Bernert was sent back to *Jasta Boelcke* to take over its leadership on June 9. He had to be relieved and went home on convalescent leave on August 18. His condition did not improve and he lingered for over a year, finally succumbing on October

18, 1918, a victim of the 'flu epidemic that was then sweeping the world.

[39] Bethge scored his 20th and last victory on March 10, 1918. His name was immediately put forward for a *Pour le Mérite*. Veteran pilots of his seniority were often nominated for the award as soon as their scores reached the magic mark of 20. Newcomers who had piled up their scores more rapidly often had to wait a while longer and had scores well over 20 when their awards came. Before Bethge's proposal could be acted upon, he was killed over Passchendale on March 17 in Pfalz D.III 5888/17. He was the first of six German fighter pilots killed before their nominations for the award could be acted upon. None of the six ever received the order posthumously.

[40] According to the authors of the comprehensively researched book. "Above the Trenches," Buddecke was the victim of Capt. Arthur T. Whealy of No. 3 Squadron, RNAS. Whealy, who was eventually accorded 27 victories (17

The customary flowers and greenery are banked around Buddecke's coffin, obscuring the lower half of his *Ordenskissen*. Other photographs taken on this occasion show a curious fact. For some reason only one of his Turkish awards was on display. Buddecke earned six Turkish awards, the Imtiaz Medal with Clasp and Sabers in Gold and in Silver, the Liakat Medal with Clasp and Sabers in Gold and in Silver, the War Medal and the Turkish Pilot's Badge. But only the War Medal was present. Buddecke is believed to be the only German airmen to receive both the Imtiaz and Liakat Medals in Gold.

Two St. Henry winners in *Flieger-Abteilung 22* on the Russian Front in 1917. *Rittmeister* Viktor Stresemann, seated 2nd from left, the *Abteilungsführer*, hosts the farewell party for *Rittm. Prinz* Friedrich Sigismund, seated 4th from the left with moustache. Stresemann, as an *Oberleutnant*, received his Knight's Cross on January 12, 1916 when with *FFL.Abt. 59*. The Prince's award was made on December 3, 1917 as a member of *Fl.Abt. 22*. Standing at the right is *Oblt.* Karl *Ritter* von Gruny who as an infantry officer won the Knight's Cross of Bavaria's highest military honor, the Military Max-Joseph Order, on October 25, 1914, thus earning personal nobility and the title of *Ritter* von.

LEUTNANT HANS-JOACHIM VON SEYDLITZ-GERSTENBERG

Awarded the Knight's Cross of the Military St. Henry Order on April 8, 1916 when serving in *Feldflieger-Abteilung 23.*

Citation: *"Lt.* von Seydlitz-Gerstenberg had already been seriously wounded earlier in a flight against the enemy but being an officer of extrordinary daring, he executed a night attack on February 20, 1916 after recovering from his injuries, flying a large 'battle plane' over enemy positions at Amiens where he bravely and coolly dropped 140 kg. of explosives in spite of heavy anti-aircraft fire and interference from search-lights, achieving great results."

Nothing more is known of this raid but von Seydlitz-Gerstenberg was obviously using one of *Feldflieger-Abteilung 23's* large A.E.G. G-Type bombers for his attack. By November 1916 he had transferred to a "Giant" airplane detachment and was with *Riesenflugzeug-Abteilung 501* on the Eastern Front. One typical mission in which he participated was a daylight bombing raid on a Russian troop encampment at Iza on November 26. It is fully described in the definitive work on these huge German aircraft, "The German Giants" by P. M. Grosz and G. W. Haddow. *Rfa 501* remained in the east until the early summer of 1917 when it returned to the Döberitz and Staaken bases near Berlin to train on the new Staaken R.VI planes. The unit moved to Belgium in August 1917 and in conjunction with *Kagohl 3* (later *Bogohl 3*) began night raids on England as well as attacks on French ports and other conventional targets on the continent.

On the night of February 16/17, 1918 von Seydlitz-Gerstenberg was the commander of the R.12 when it and a sister ship, the R.39, from a flight of five of them penetrated the London defences. The R.39 was carrying the first 1,000 kilogram bomb to be dropped on England. It hit the Royal Chelsea Hospital, killing five people and doing extensive damage. The R.12's smaller bombs fell on Woolwich where seven died. During his run, von Seydlitz-Gerstenberg's plane flew right into the balloon apron that stretched between the Woolwich Works and the West India Docks. The impact threw the R.12 first to the right, then to the left and finally it went into a slide-slip to the left, falling out of control. By a deft bit of engine manip-

ulation the pilot, a *Leutnant* Götte, righted the air-craft. It flew on with only minor actual damage.

For a man who had had such a close call as that and who had risked his life on many other occasions, his end was not what such a stout (literally as well as figuratively) warrior would have wished. On July 26, 1918 he was killed when a conventional two-seater, possibly the squadron transport or "hack," in which he was flying crashed at Scheldewindeke near Ghent.

The May 15, 1915 issue of *Flugsport* noted that von Seydlitz-Gerstenberg had been awarded the Albert Order, Knight 2nd Class with Swords as a member of *Feldflieger-Abteilung 23.* This is confirmed on the roll with, however, the usual late posting. The date there is July 15, 1915.

HAUPTMANN ERNST KUNZ

Awarded the Knight's Cross of the Military St. Henry Order on April 14, 1916 when serving in *Feldflieger-Abteilung 33.*

Citation: "As an observer, *Hptm.* Kunz has proved himself as a brave and daring officer. In a successful air battle that one of the Fokker machines of his detachment had with an English biplane behind enemy lines on January 17, 1916, because of his excellent directives his pilot was able to escape from the enemy plane."

The *Militär-Wochenblatt* of January 27, 1915 listed Kunz, then an *Oberleutnant* in a unit not specified, as a recipient of the Albert Order, Knight 2nd Class with Swords. This award does not appear on the roll until November 1, 1915. His rank there is *Hauptmann* and his unit is given as *Feldflieger-Abteilung 29.*

LEUTNANT KARL BIRCH-HIRSCHFELD

Awarded the Knight's Cross of the Military St. Henry Order on May 26, 1916 when serving in *Kampfstaffel 9* of *Kampfgeschwader 2.*

Citation: "On May 2, 1916 *Lt.* Birch-Hirschfeld came to the aid of another aircraft of his battle squadron over an enemy position north of Verdun. The other aircraft was in a difficult combat with three Caudrons and two Nieuports. Together they shot down one of the Nieuports.

The *Feldflieger-Abteilung 23* arm patch clearly shows on the left sleeve of *Leutnant* Hans-Joachim von Seydlitz-Gerstenberg's tunic as he cradles a squadron puppy at tea time in the unit. He received the Knight's Cross of the Military St. Henry Order on April 8, 1916 with the unit. Others are, left to right: *Oblt.* Trentpohl, *Oblt.* Berthold, a visiting war artist, possibly the *Flak Offizier* Worth and *Unteroffz.* Margot.

A "Giant" airplane of *Riesenflugzeug-Abteilung 501,* von Seydlitz-Gerstenberg's later unit, provides a dramatic backdrop to his funeral ceremonies. He was killed on July 26, 1918 in a crash of a conventional two-seater. Unfortunately, the photograph is not sharp enough to make out what appear to be as many as seven awards on the *Ordenskissen* being held by the man at the extreme left.

Since he joined the squadron in September 1915, *Lt.* Birch-Hirschfeld has distinguished himself through great aggressiveness and coolness in difficult phases of the air war."

Still with *Kasta 9* of *Kagohl 2 Lt.* Birch-Hirschfeld and his pilot, *Lt.* Friedrich Rudolph Heinemann, were killed over Virginy in the Argonne on March 18, 1917 when they collided in mid-air with the Nieuport of a *Caporal* Hofman of *Escadrille N.80.*

No other awards for Birch-Hirschfeld have been found. Although he had pre-air service in Royal Saxon *Infanterie-Regiment Nr. 107,* he was a native of Hesse. Thus, like the Prussians Berthold and Buddecke, it is possible he held no other Saxon awards other than the Knight's St. Henry.

LEUTNANT REINOLD HULTZSCH

Awarded the Knight's Cross of the Military St. Henry Order on May 29, 1916 when serving in *Artillerie-Flieger-Abteilung 210.*

Citation: "Despite heavy enemy defensive fire, *Lt.* Hultzsch, as an observer, took 11 photographs of enemy batteries in the 23rd Infantry Division's sector on March 31, 1916. This was a result long sought by the 23rd's Field Artillery Brigade. Enemy fire forced him back four times. However, he managed to remain over the position until his mission was completed. The aircraft returned heavily damaged by 42 hits. On April 3, *Lt.* Hultzsch repeatedly attacked several enemy biplanes, forcing them back from our front. By his exemplary bravery in the days following the storming of the heights at La Ville aux Bois on March 10 and in the reconnaissances of the shifting artillery positions, *Lt.* Hultzsch rendered extraordinary service for the 23rd's Field Artillery Brigade north of Reims."

On August 18, 1916, Hultzsch and his pilot, *Unteroffizier* Eugen Grützbach, still with *Artillerie-Flieger-Abteilung 210,* fell in action near Foure aux Wald northwest of Cambrai.

This was the first award of a Knight's St. Henry to a man in an *Artillerie-Flieger-Abteilung,* a unit specifically assigned artillery cooperation duties. Earlier, Hultzsch had received the Albert Order, Knight 2nd Class with Swords. This was noted in

the April 12, 1916 issue of *Flugsport* and for once it is entered on the roll with an earlier date, this being January 20, 1916.

OBERLEUTNANT ERNST SIEVERTS

Awarded the Knight's Cross of the Military St. Henry Order on May 29, 1916 when serving in *Feldflieger-Abteilung 62.*

Citation: "*Oblt.* Sieverts carried out many successful wartime flights and displayed great nerve, daring and bravery in many air battles. His reports and photographs, taken at low altitude and under heavy defensive fire, were an important service to the Troop. On March 30, 1916, after a difficult air combat, he forced an English biplane down near Wancourt, southeast of Arras, and the crew was taken prisoner."

The Royal Flying Corps Communique for March 30, 1916 reads in part:

"Two machines on photographic duty, one of 11 Sqn (pilot, 2 Lt Castle, observer 2 AM Coleman) and one of 15 Sqn (pilot, 2 Lt J. G. Welsford, observer, 2 Lt W. Joyce) were also brought down. The first was seen to fall in flames between Fampoux and Monchy le Preux, and 2 Lt Welsford is believed to have been killed in the second, which fell in the same neighbourhood."

Wancourt is just several miles south of Monchy le Preux with Fampoux to the north of Monchy le Preux. It seems likely, therefore, that one of these two British losses was the plane shot down by Sieverts' gun (he was the observer), probably the aircraft of Welsford and Joyce inasmuch as the other one was shot down in flames which almost always doomed the unfortunate crew.

No published sources found to date mention other awards to Sieverts but from the studio portrait of him we can see that, at least up to that time, he had earned, in addition to his Knight's St. Henry, the Albert Order, Knight 2nd Class with Swords, both Iron Crosses and the Hamburg Hanseatic Cross. He is also wearing his Imperial German Army Air Service Observer's Badge and the Austro-Hungarian Field Pilot's Badge in the Franz-Joseph pattern.

Oberleutnant Dr. Sieverts

(Above)
Natural foliage and potted plants are banked
on the coffin of *Leutnant* Reinold Hultzsch
who was killed in action on August 18, 1916 as
a member of *Artillerie-Flieger-Abteilung 210.*
He had earned the Knight's Cross of the Military St. Henry Order the previous May 29.
The plaque with a stylized Iron Cross states
that he died a hero's death for the Fatherland.

(To the Left)
A fine portrait photograph of a rather cadaver-
ous *Oberleutnant Dr.* Ernst Sieverts in full
regalia from one of the patriotic postcards of
war heroes that became so popular in Germany during the war. Sieverts received his
Knight's St. Henry in *Feldflieger-Abteilung 62*
on the same date as Hultzsch's award, May
29, 1916.

LEUTNANT PHILIPP FRANKE

Awarded the Knight's Cross of the Military St. Henry Order on June 13, 1916 when serving in *Artillerie-Flieger-Abteilung 201*.

Citation: "*Lt.* Francke, who had already fought several air battles during reconnaissance flights, distinguished himself during the January 28, 1916 "Rupprecht Undertaking" and the May 25, 1916 "Holstein Undertaking" - the storming of the enemy trenches near Givenchy. Both times, due to poor weather and low visibility, he was forced to cross the lines at low altitude. As a result he was able to locate the fire of the enemy batteries and quickly report to his own artillery, permitting them to counter effectively. He contributed to the success of the undertakings and the minimizing of our losses."

Franke's award of the Albert Order, Knight 2nd Class with Swords while a member of *Artillerie-Flieger-Abteilung 201* shows up on the roll dated February 28, 1916 and found its way into an announcement of it in *Flugsport* in the issue of May 24, 1916.

OBERLEUTNANT ERWIN HAUCKE

Awarded the Knight's Cross of the Military St. Henry Order on June 13, 1916 when serving in *Artillerie-Flieger-Abteilung 219*.

Citation: "*Oblt.* Haucke's service as an observer during the battle of (Lake) Narocz was especially important to the Troop, particularly during the attack on April 28, 1916. Despite the bad weather and heavy fire, he succeeded in directing our artillery against the superior enemy artillery batteries. On the day of the attack, *Oblt.* Haucke, through his wireless telegraphy reports, made possible the storming of infantry positions, the crippling of the enemy artillery and the disposition of troops from the concentration points for attacks on enemy reserves and ammunition columns. *Oblt.* Haucke's contribution is particularly significant because he was not deterred by enemy fire and the several hits to his machine."

OBERLEUTNANT WILHELM HAUPT

Awarded the Knight's Cross of the Military St. Henry Order on June 13, 1916 when serving in *Feldflieger-Abteilung 47*.

Citation: "*Oblt.* Haupt caused major damage to the railroad station at Epernay with two bombs on the afternoon of April 29, 1916. At dawn on May 18 he flew over the Russian camp near Mailly where the Russian replacements from Marseille were quartered and successfully dropped a large bomb - this was confirmed by the foreign press. This 3½ hour flight in heavy defensive fire and against strong French air patrols over 60 km. behind enemy lines was the greatest achievement of *Oblt.* Haupt who also displayed bravery and skill in his regular missions as an observer."

An *Oberleutnant* Wilhelm Haupt is shown on the roll of the Merit Order as receiving the Knight 2nd Class with Swords on March 16, 1917. His unit is given as *Flieger-Abteilung 30* whose previous designation was *Feldflieger-Abteilung 30 (Feldflieger-Abteilung 47's* later designation was *Flieger-Abteilung 6)*. In the absence of further information on other units in which Haupt may have served in addition to *Feldflieger-Abteilung 30*, it is not possible to say whether we are talking about the same man. If it were, then undoubtedly the date on the roll is another late posting since a Saxon like Haupt would normally have received the Merit Order ahead of the St. Henry (and he would also have possessed the Albert Order since there is no known instance where a holder of a Knight's grade of the Merit Order did not also have the Albert).

LEUTNANT HERBERT KETTNER

Awarded the Knight's Cross of the Military St. Henry Order on June 22, 1916 when serving in *Kampfstaffel 25* of *Kampfgeschwader 5*.

Citation: "*Lt.* Kettner carried out many successful air battles as an observer. On May 20, 1916, he and his pilot attacked an enemy squadron of seven aircraft. After a long fight they forced one enemy aircraft to crash. The others fled."

LEUTNANT HANS THÜMMLER

Awarded the Knight's Cross of the Military St. Henry Order on June 22, 1916 when serving in *Artillerie-Flieger-Abteilung 201*.

Several officers survey the wreckage of the Staaken R.VI (Albs) 38/16 "Giant" aircraft on the morning after its crash on May 6, 1918 while other men sift through the scattered debris. The plane was on its delivery flight to *Riesen-Flugzeug-Abteilung 501* when the disaster occurred (see text for details). Seven men perished in the crash including Knight's St. Henry Cross winner, *Oberleutnant* Hans Thümmler. Thümmler had received his award on June 22, 1916 for his perseverance on a number of reconnaissance missions as an observer in *Artillerie-Flieger-Abteilung 201*.

Citation: "Through persistence and particular fearlessness, *Lt.* Thümmler succeeded in bringing back valuable reconnaissance information on days when the battle was at its most perilous. This was the basis for an effective response to the enemy artillery. On April 30, 1916, after putting an enemy aircraft to flight, he was surprised and shot up. His aircraft took 15 serious hits. Despite this, he continued the combat until the second enemy fled. *Lt.* Thümmler also carried out a notable service on May 21, 1916 near Givenchy. Despite strong defences, he reconnoitered the enemy flank protection batteries at low altitude which enabled us to counter them."

Thümmler, like his fellow St. Henry winner von Seydlitz-Gerstenberg, transferred from a conventional two-seater unit to join a "Giant" aircraft squadron. And like him, Thümmler was killed in a crash but this time in one of the R-Planes themselves. The disaster occurred on the delivery flight of the R.38 to *Riesen-Flugzeug-Abteilung 501* on May 6, 1918. The R.38 had been accepted on March 27 and was on its way to the front. Thümmler, now an *Oberleutnant*, was the ranking member of the crew and as such, may have been the aircraft commander. At any rate, it was the commander who made a fateful decision to press on with the flight when a more prudent course would have been a delay until the following morning.

The flight plan was to be from Döberitz to the Giant aircraft replacement unit at Cologne. Orders were to break the journey at Hanover if any problems in continuing on were encountered. The take-off at Döberitz had been delayed and as a result darkness was approaching as they reached Hanover. Nonetheless, they overflew the city and foolishly continued on to their final destination. As night fell the commander became disoriented. A compass heading might have brought them to the Rhine from which it would have been possible to trace the course of the river and pick up Cologne. Instead, the commander decided to take a more direct route over the Ruhr valley. Now really lost, the R.38 fired identification flares. These were answered by bursts from anti-aircraft batteries who saw the signals and attempted to show by their fire in which direction Cologne lay. The R.38 had been in the air for about five hours and fuel was running short. There was no choice but to try an emergency landing. The huge plane made a good touchdown on a rural road near the town of Heisingen an der Ruhr but a wing hooked a high-tension tower on its run. The aircraft spun and smashed into a cliff. Fire left little but skeletal remains for those who sifted through the wreckage at daylight the next morning. Killed along with Thümmler were *Leutnant* Waldemer Potemca, *Sergeant* Otto Aust, *Unteroffizier* Albert Perwas, *Gefreiter* Jakob Burgmayer, *Gefreiter* Siegfried Henning and *Flieger* Wilfried Klaunburg.

Thümmler's name appears on the roll as receiving the Albert Order, Knight 2nd Class with Swords on March 17, 1916 when in *Artillerie-Flieger-Abteilung 201*. The announcement of this appeared in the May 24, 1916 issue of *Flugsport*.

LEUTNANT WERNER PFEIL

Awarded the Knight's Cross of the Military St. Henry Order on July 3, 1916 when serving in *Feld-flieger-Abteilung 59*.

Citation: "*Lt.* Pfeil, who joined the air service after being badly wounded in August 1914, had many successful war flights in the eastern and western theaters of operation. On February 19, 1916 he badly damaged the rail yards and the locomotive of a Russian transport train in a night bombing attack on Tarnopol, as was confirmed voluntarily by prisoners. On April 1 he took excellent photographs of a Russian position. His life was endangered by enemy artillery thereby. A hit went straight through the rudder."

According to the roll, Pfeil received the Albert Order, Knight 2nd Class with Swords on March 14, 1916 while in *Feldflieger-Abteilung 59*. An announcement to this effect appeared in the May 24, 1916 issue of *Flugsport*.

OBERLEUTNANT LOTHAR WILISCH

Awarded the Knight's Cross of the Military St. Henry Order on July 22, 1916 when serving in *Feldflieger-Abteilung 24*.

Citation: "*Oblt.* Wilisch distinguished himself in ranging by wireless telegraphy against a special 30.5 cm. gun near Touquet-Parmentier for the 6th Battery of the 19th Foot Artillery Regiment and against a 20.4 cm. gun at Erguinghem near Armentieres on May 5, 1916. Because of poor visibility, he had to fly continuously over the objectives for 2½ hours, drawing fire especially from the first mentioned gun. The aircraft was twice attacked by enemy biplanes. Each time *Oblt.* Wilisch fired with his machine gun and forced the opponents back, the second one into a steep glide in order to escape. After a short refueling stop, *Oblt.* Wilisch took off to go after the second gun. Thanks to his bravery and perseverance, both weapons were silenced for a long time."

Wilisch was also a recipient of the Albert Order, Knight 2nd Class with Swords but here again we find a considerable discrepancy between the date of award as carried on the roll versus its actual receipt. The roll carries the entry of June 30, 1915 while Wilisch actually received the award on December 9, 1914 in *Feldflieger-Abteilung 24.*

RITTMEISTER WERNER *FREIHERR* VON BESCHWITZ

Awarded the Knight's Cross of the Military St. Henry Order on August 3, 1916 when serving in *Feldflieger-Abteilung 39.*

Citation: *"Rittmeister Freiherr* von Beschwitz led *Feldflieger-Abt. 39* of the *XVIII. A.K.* since May 31, 1916. He proved himself to be a distinguished and brave flier. On the night of July 1 and 2 over Laon he was attacked by an overwhelming enemy force and successfully fought them off. In the landing after this difficult night flight he was seriously injured."

LEUTNANT GEORG VON ZOBEL

Awarded the Knight's Cross of the Military St. Henry Order on September 12, 1916 when serving in *Feldflieger-Abteilung 39.*

Citation: "On his many reconnaissance flights since July 1916, *Lt.* von Zobel showed courage, decisiveness and tactical insight. The Chief of Field Aviation gave him special recognition for an aerial victory on July 26."

The roll shows the award of the Albert Order, Knight 2nd Class with Swords to von Zobel on May 16, 1916 as a member of *Feldflieger-Abteilung 39.* The announcement of the award appeared in *Flugsport* in its August 2, 1916 issue.

OBERLEUTNANT FRIEDRICH KNAB

Awarded the Knight's Cross of the Military St.

Henry Order on September 23, 1916 when serving in *Kampfgeschwader 5.*

Citation: *"Oblt.* Knab flew numerous important reconnaissance missions, distinguishing himself in several air combats through courage and good judgment. On May 7, 1916 he prevented the penetration of an enemy squadron in a decisive engagement on the east banks of the Maas during the course of the Battle of Verdun. After a long fight, he caused one of the aircraft to crash in flames."

Earlier, Knab had served in *Feldflieger-Abteilung 23* where, according to the roll, he received the Albert Order, Knight 2nd Class with Swords on January 11, 1916.

OBERLEUTNANT HANS BALDAMUS

Awarded the Knight's Cross of the Military St. Henry Order on September 26, 1916 when serving in *Artillerie-Flieger-Abteilung 201.*

Citation: *"Oblt.* Baldamus was with *Art.-Flieg.-Abt. 201* in July and August 1916 which was in the sector that included the 6th Bavarian Reserve Division and which was under heavy attack. On July 19, while flying at 400 meters due to poor visibility, he spotted numerous enemy batteries which made their engagement possible. On August 28, 1916 during the great battle, he also succeeded in locating 15 enemy batteries and three heavy guns that were firing which enabled their successful engagement. These two reconnaissance flights proved his courage and prowess as an observer."

On December 11, 1916 Baldamus' two-seater Albatros was brought down by anti-aircraft fire along the British frontline trenches near Beauraine, a few kilometers south of Arras. His pilot, *Flieger* Herbert Ruwe, was killed and Baldamus was taken prisoner. In the book "Above the Trenches" six pilots of No. 60 Squadron, RFC are said to have shared in this victory. It is believed, however, that the Albatros two-seater they brought down was one that was crewed by *Unteroffizier* Rücke (pilot) and *Leutnant* Scholz (observer) and that it fell at Dainville on the western outskirts of Arras. Capt. Eustace O. Grenfull, one of the British pilots credited with a victory for this engagement and whose eighth and last confirmed victory it was,

Three members of *Flieger-Abteilung (A)211* in the summer of 1917. Left to right, *Oberleutnant* Wagner, *Leutnant* Walter and *Leutnant* Martin Möbius. Möbius received the Knight's Cross of the Military St. Henry Order on June 22, 1917 for a number of successful flights during the Battle of Arras that spring and especially for bringing his burning plane down safely after an air combat on April 22 in which he was lightly wounded. He joined *Jasta 7* as a fighter pilot on January 18, 1918 but lost his life only six days later in a mid-air collision with an S.E.5a that he was attacking.

Often, it seems, the ever-present squadron puppy bore an uncanny resemblance to his master. Here with friend is *Leutnant* Kurt Schneider, an original member of *Jagdstaffel 5* who scored a total of 15 confirmed victories before he was fatally wounded in an air battle on July 14, 1917. Ten days later he was awarded the St. Henry Knight's Cross posthumously.

collided with a British plane in an air combat over Becelaere, apparently Lt. A. W. Morey of No. 60 Squadron, RFC flying S.E.5a B.4897. Both men were killed. Jacobs later wrote that Möbius died in scoring what would have been his second victory. The *Nachrichtenblatt* gives no such credit to Möbius that day nor is there any earlier entry in those reports that would have established a first confirmed victory for him.

LEUTNANT WERNER ROLOFF

Awarded the Knight's Cross of the Military St. Henry Order on June 22, 1917 when serving in *Flieger-Abteilung (A)211*.

Citation: "*Lt.* Roloff carried out brave and distinguished flights as an infantry cooperation flier in the 1916 Battle of the Somme and the spring battles near Arras in April 1917, bringing back important information for headquarters. He fought many bitter aerial combats; for example: on May 9, 1917 he attacked an enemy observation balloon and in the ensuing brave strike at it forced the crew to abandon the balloon."

The *Nachrichtenblatt* gives no credit for any balloons destroyed on the Western Front on May 9, 1917. Perhaps Roloff was unable to burn the gas bag after the crew took to their parachutes and unless a balloon was torched, no confirmation for a victory was forthcoming.

LEUTNANT WALTER KÖHLER

Awarded the Knight's Cross of the Military St. Henry Order on July 16, 1917 when serving in *Flieger-Abteilung 3*.

Citation: "*Lt.* Köhler flew on many missions deep into enemy territory, to Calais and St. Omer, returning with important reconnaissance information. In all his flights he displayed decisiveness and good judgment. Coming back from a flight on June 12, 1917, he was attacked in the clouds by three Belgian single-seater fighters behind the Belgian front lines. He was severely wounded by two shots in the elbow. With great care he directed the pilot deep behind the German lines whereupon the badly shot up machine cartwheeled on landing. With great presence of mind. *Lt.* Köhler took valuable photographs which he brought back home safely

despite his serious injury."

HAUPTMANN GERT-WOLF FROEHLICH

Awarded the Knight's Cross of the Military St. Henry Order on July 24, 1917 when serving in *Flieger-Abteilung (A)226*.

Citation: "*Hptm.* Froehlich flew on the Somme from March 1916 to February 1917, fighting through the entire Battle of the Somme. Although twice wounded in an air battle on June 22, 1916, he directed the artillery ranging on an enemy battery. From September 1916 on, he flew with success in the battles at Combles, Rancourt, Bouchavesnes and Sailly-Saillisel, carrying out special orders from the Chief of Staff of Army Group C as well as flying several times a day on artillery and infantry cooperation work. From January 1917 on, *Hptm.* Froehlich was the leader of *Fliegerabteilung (A)226*, on the Somme until the end of February and then on the Aisne in the dual battle of Aisne-Champagne. With exceptional bravery *Hptm.* Froehlich distinguished himself on all his flights."

Froehlich died in unknown circumstances, one source stating the date was November 30, 1918, the other stating it was December 1, 1918.

LEUTNANT MARTIN HEYDRICH

Awarded the Knight's Cross of the Military St. Henry Order on July 24, 1917 when serving in *Schutzstaffel 11*.

Citation: "*Lt.* Heydrich flew many combat missions around Verdun, in the Battle of the Somme in 1916 and the battle near Arras in the spring of 1917. He shot down an opponent on the Somme. On January 25 and February 10, 1917 he dropped bombs on Albert and Frichicourt. On February 11, 1917, far behind enemy lines, he forced an enemy balloon to be pulled down in repeated attacks. On the same flight he withstood a severe attack by an enemy squadron. He fought with ability and courage and did not break off until his machine was hit several times."

The *Nachrichtenblatt* lists no enemy balloons destroyed on February 11, 1917 so, as the citation suggests, Heydrich's target was apparently winched down intact.

The roll of the Merit Order lists Heydrich's name as receiving the Knight 2nd Class with Swords on December 1, 1916 as a member of *Kampfstaffel 29* of *Kampfgeschwader 5*. This unit became *Schutzstaffel 11* in the reorganization of flying units that occurred in the fall of 1916. The *Kagohl* were reduced to three in number and the *Kasta* thus freed by this reduction were used to form 30 *Schutzstaffeln*. The *Schusta* were to provide defense for the two-seaters of the *Flieger-Abteilungen* and, increasingly, to engage in infantry cooperation work through offensive support operations of their own.[58] It can be assumed that, earlier, Heydrich was also awarded the Albert Order, Knight 2nd Class with Swords but the date so far has not surfaced.

LEUTNANT KURT SCHNEIDER

Awarded the Knight's Cross of the Military St. Henry Order posthumously on July 24, 1917 after serving in *Jagdstaffel 5*.

Citation: "*Lt.* Schneider, who had already distinguished himself at Verdun and in the Battle of the Somme with brilliant bravery and complete enthusiasm, downed 12 aircraft and three tethered balloons in the period March 19 to May 28, 1917. On June 5 he was severely wounded in an air battle. In him the section lost their bravest and most proved pilot. He was no longer alive when awarded the high decoration."

The citation implies that Schneider's June 5 wounding was fatal. It was not. Although the wound, a shot in the thigh, was serious, Schneider returned to duty only to suffer another wound in an aerial combat on July 14, 1917. He died the same day despite emergency treatment. So the citation is right in this respect; Schneider never lived to wear the high award.

Schneider was one of the original pilots of *Jasta 5* when it was formed out of *Kampfeinsitzer-Kommando-Ost (Avillers)* on August 21, 1916. Just four days earlier his Pilot's Badge had been officially authorized and he already wore the Iron Cross, 2nd Class which he had earned on March 15, 1915. *Jasta 5* was under the command of *Oberleutnant* Hans Berr.[59] Typical of the early days of these all-fighter formations, the unit was originally equipped with a mixed bag of aircraft. On charge as *Jasta 5* began its patrols were the old Fokker E.III monoplane which had as yet not been totally replaced and newer biplane types, the Fokker D.III, the Halberstadt D.II and the Roland D.I.

Although he had yet to score a confirmed victory, Schneider's service was recognized with the award of the Albert Order, Knight 2nd Class with Swords which he received on January 13, 1917 (the date on the roll is January 10). Schneider broke the ice when he downed an F.E.2b on March 17. Two days later he was credited with a Spad. The March 17 victory was not confirmed until later which must have accounted for the fact that the citation puts the start of his victory string as the 19th of March, not the 17th. An enemy biplane of a type not identified became his next victim on April 12. The following morning at 9:00 a.m. two more F.E.s, these of the "d" model, fell almost simultaneously under his guns. Victories numbered six and seven were balloons destroyed on April 22. Two other fast rising stars of *Jasta 5*, *Leutnant* Heinrich Gontermann and *Offizier-Stellvertreter* Edmund Nathanael, also burned balloons that day on either side of Schneider's attacks and for good measure, Nathanael added a Spad to his score in the waning hours of that evening.[60]

---

[58] In March 1918, in order to describe their offensive role in supporting the infantry more accurately, the 38 *Schusta* that were in existence at the time were renamed *Schlachtstaffeln (Schlasta)*.

[59] Berr would earn the *Orden Pour le Mérite* on December 4, 1916 after reaching 10 victories. He was killed in a mid-air collision with a wingmate in a combat on April 6, 1917 with his victory score still standing at 10.

[60] Gontermann joined *Jasta 5* on November 9, 1916 and by the end of April 1917 he had an official score of 16 victories. This fine record was rewarded with a command of his own and on April 30 he took over *Jasta 15*. After scoring his 21st victory, he was awarded the *Orden Pour le Mérite* on May 14.

By October 2 his record of victories reached 39. Gontermann was a balloon specialist. Seventeen of his victories were over these heavily defended and thus highly dangerous targets. On October 29, 1917 Gontermann took up one of the Fokker Triplanes, Dr.1 115/17, for a test flight. The upper wing collapsed and he crashed heavily and died of his injuries the next day.

Nathanael joined *Jasta 5* at the beginning of March 1917 and promptly scored his first victory on March 6. He had had a distinguished record in *Feldflieger-Abteilung 42* where he had been decorated with two exclusive awards from the Grand Duchy of Saxe-Weimar in 1916, the General Honor Decoration in Gold with Swords and the Wilhelm Ernst War

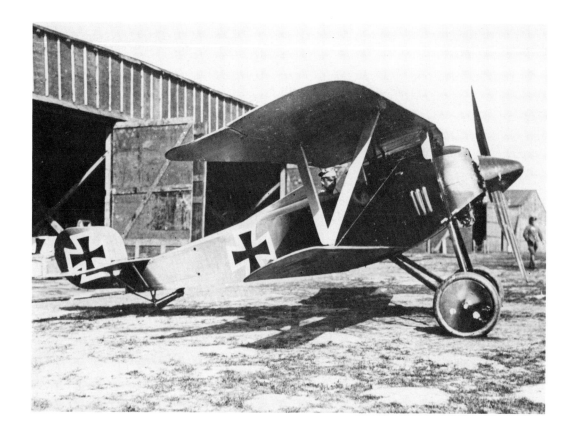

Leutnant Kurt (sometimes spelled Curt) Schneider was the third man in a
Jagdstaffel to receive the Military St. Henry Order. In the photograph above he
poses in the cockpit of an S.S.W. D.I wearing his service cap. Note the replacement
wing stashed in one of Jasta 5's distinctive wooden hangers. Now bareheaded,
Schneider again poses for the camera, this time in his Albatros. Someone forgot to
remove the step ladder before the shutter was snapped!

"Somewhere in Palestine." *Leutnant* Kurt Fritzsche (left) and his observer. *Lt.* Schmarje, pose atop the fuselage of their Rumpler C.I in *Flieger-Abteilung 300 "Pascha."* The crew was credited with shooting down British aircraft on February 28 and July 13, 1917. Fritzsche received the Knight's Cross of the Military St. Henry Order while still with the unit on September 21, 1917.

By the time *Leutnant* Hans-Gottfried von Haebler's Knight's St. Henry Order caught up with him on October 2, 1917 he was a fighter pilot in *Jagdstaffel 36* although the award came for a valuable long-range reconnaissance flight he and his observer made the previous month with *Flieger-Abteilung (A)273*. With eight victories, seven of which were officially confirmed, von Haebler's triplane was hit by ground fire near Bapaume on March 22, 1918 and he died in British lines.

importance of the reconnaissance but also from a technological standpoint of the time. It could only have been accomplished by great energy. *Lt.* von Haebler made it possible for his observer officer to take 50 photographs, giving a complete overview of the front from Reims to the Swiss border."

This significant feat took place on September 10, 1917. Immediately thereafter (possibly because of it?), von Haebler transferred to fighters and after a quick conversion course, reported to his new assignment, *Jagdstaffel 36,* on September 30. Thus he was already in a single-seater formation when his long range mission in *(A)273* was rewarded with the Knight's St. Henry. *Jasta 36* was located up in Flanders where there was plenty of action and von Haebler was immediately in the thick of things.

It took only a week for von Haebler to post his first victory, a Bristol "Fighter" that went down over Menin on October 7. Two more successes followed before the month was out, a Sopwith single-seater on the 12th and a Camel in flames over Houthoulst Forest on the 27th. There was only a lone victory in November as the weather turned, either an S.E.5 or another Sopwith on the 4th. Von Haebler closed out his eventful 1917 with twin kills on December 8, one more Camel and an R.E.8.

After some well deserved leave in late January and February, von Haebler was back in action in March of the new year and got his seventh confirmed victory on March 8 and his eighth on March 18, both Sopwith Camels. *Jasta 36* was now a part of *Jagdgeschwader 3* which had been formed on February 1, 1918 and which also comprised *Jasta Boelcke, 26* and *27.* All three *Jagdgeschwadern* (*Jagdgeschwader 2* had also been formed on February 1 and consisted of *Jasta 12, 13, 15* and *19*) were using the Fokker Triplane now (the first *Jagdgeschwader* had been created on June 23, 1917 by combining *Jasta 4, 6, 10* and *11*). So it was that von Haebler was in his Fokker Dr.1 509/17 on a combat patrol over Bapaume on March 22. Just the day before the Germans had launched their massive drive along a 50-mile front against the British Third and Fourth Armies which was designed to split the British and French, roll the British up to the Channel and win a decision in the west before America's manpower and materiel could tip the scales against Germany forever. Von Haebler's aircraft was hit by ground fire and

brought down in British lines. The very next day, March 24, Bapaume was overrun by the rapidly advancing German storm troopers and the remains of von Haebler's triplane were found, reasonably intact apparently. There was hope that he might have survived and was a prisoner. He had indeed been taken but had died of his injuries on the 22nd.

Once again, photographs supply the information on his other awards. In addition to his Knight's St. Henry, he received the Knight 2nd Class with Swords of both the Merit and Albert Orders, both Iron Crosses and the Knight's Cross with Swords of the Royal Hohenzollern House Order.

LEUTNANT JOHANNES ZIEGLER

Awarded the Knight's Cross of the Military St. Henry Order on October 2, 1917 when serving in *Flieger-Abteilung (A)273.*

Citation: (Ziegler was von Haebler's observer on their long range reconnaissance on September 10, 1917. The citation for Ziegler's award is virtually identical to von Haebler's)

Ziegler was a native Saxon, born in Leipzig, the kingdom's second city, and was relatively old for a flier. He had just celebrated his 30th birthday the month before the mission in question (von Haebler was a more typical 22 years old). The *Nachrichtenblatt* of September 20, 1917 singled out their feat with the following statement:

"Enemy Flight of 360 Km.

The *Lts.* v. Haebler and Ziegler of *Fl.A. (A)273* flew 360 km. behind French lines on 10.9 over Reims - Chalons - Langres - Belfort and Southern Alsace in an almost five hour flight, bringing back important photographs.

The Supreme Commander of the 3rd Army has given his special recognition to the crew."

LEUTNANT WALTER VON BÜLOW

Awarded the Knight's Cross of the Military St. Henry Order on October 7, 1918 (sic?) when serving in *Jagdstaffel 36.*

Citation: "*Lt.* von Bülow, who enlisted in the Royal

The two von Bülow brothers who served together in *Jasta 36*, the 28-victory *Pour le Mérite* ace Walter on the left and the six-victory flier Harry on the right. One of them received the Military St. Henry Order (see text for the contradictions in the citation). As well as other evidence, these two photographs strongly suggest it was Walter who received the Knight's Cross of the order, not Harry. The third ribbon on the bar Walter is wearing on his 17th Brunswick "Death's Head" Hussar tunic here gives every appearance of being the St. Henry Order. The photograph of Harry was taken sometime after October 9, 1918, the date of his award of the Knight's Cross with Swords of the Royal Hohenzollern House Order (here worn through a frog on his hussar tunic). The date of the award of the St. Henry in the citation is October 7, 1918 (but probably it actually was October 7, 1917). Had Harry been the one to receive it, he would certainly have been wearing at least the ribbon for it here. His bar shows ribbons for the Iron Cross, 2nd Class, the Brunswick War Merit Cross, 2nd Class and the Albert Order, Knight 2nd Class with Swords. He received the latter award on May 3, 1917 as a member of *Flieger-Abteilung (A)272*.

Saxon Hussar Regiment No. 18 as a volunteer in 1915, was transferred to the air service at his own request. He led a flight in *Jagdstaffel 36* in a courageous and competent manner. On May 8, 1918 he met the famous Captain Clerk (sic) in the air, forcing him to land behind our own lines after a difficult combat.[63] Through his talents as a flier, exemplary skill and leadership qualities, he succeeded in leading the section to its fullest capabilities. The command of the unit was given to him in June 1918 as a result of his achievements. On July 15, 1918 *Staffel 36* had its 100th aerial victory. *Lt.* von Bülow's personal contribution was six victories. The high decoration came after he was no longer alive."

There is much confusion here. The citation mentions Walter von Bülow by name yet everything said therein except for the last sentence concerning the fact that he was no longer alive to receive the Knight's St. Henry in person refers not to Walter, but to his younger brother, Harry. Both served in *Jasta 36* with Walter as its Commanding Officer from May 15, 1917 until December 12, 1917 and Harry as its leader from May 27, 1918 until August 14, 1918. Harry survived the war but Walter was killed in action on January 6, 1918, having been switched from the command of *Jasta 36* to that of *Jasta Boelcke.* So how are we to determine just which of the two was the recipient of the Military St. Henry Order? The matter could be settled with certainty if their respective service records were at hand but so far, efforts to find them have not been successful. However, there is compelling evidence from other sources that it was Walter, not Harry, who received the award.

The most definitive word on the matter comes from Harry himself. In a letter to an historian in this country in 1973 when he was still alive, Harry listed his brother's awards and included the Knight's Cross of the order. Contemporary photographs also support this conclusion (see the captions under the photographs of the two brothers that appear here). If all the evidence points, therefore, to Walter receiving the award and not Harry, then the stated bestowal date of October 7, 1918

may have been a typographical error and should have read October 7, 1917. On the basis that Walter was, in fact, the recipient of the order, a brief account of his wartime service is given here.

Walter von Bülow's frontline air service began when he joined *Feldflieger-Abteilung 22* in September 1915 after active duty with *Braunschweigisches Husaren-Regiment Nr. 17,* the famous "Death's Head" unit whose frogged tunic and skull and crossbones device on the service cap he continued to wear.[64] Between flying the A.E.G. "large battle planes" which was the primary equipment of his new unit, he also piloted one of the *Eindeckers* that were on charge for protection work. It is believed that von Bülow scored his first two victories during his stint with *Feldflieger-Abteilung 22,* the first of which may have been on October 10, 1915 when a French aircraft was downed in the Champagne where von Bülow was stationed. He was next shipped to the east and joined *Flieger-Abteilung 300 "Pascha"* in Palestine. Here, too, he flew fighters in support of the unit's two-seaters. It is likely that he scored two victories in this theater as well. An unofficial source mentions one on August 2, 1916 in the Sinai and another on September 16 near El Arish. He returned to the Western Front wearing the Turkish War Medal for his efforts and joined *Jasta 18* on December 7, 1916. From that point on in his career his remaining victories appear in the official *Nachrichtenblatt.*

The debut of the then 22-year old hussar in his new assignment was quite auspicious. On January 23, 1917 he shot down his fifth and sixth confirmed victories. One was identified with the generic term "Vickers" and the other either a Sopwith according to one source or an F.E.8 according to another. He added a Sopwith 1½ Strutter only three days later and then slowed down a bit with one victory in each of the following two months. Another 1½ Strutter was credited to him on February 7 and on March 11 he destroyed a new type of target, an observation balloon. April was busier. The important mark of 10 confirmed victories was reached on April 7 when he downed an F.E.2d. By this time the old standard of six victories before a fighter

---

[63] The pilot in question was Capt. Cecil C. Clark of No. 1 Squadron, RAF. He was shot down by *Leutnant* Harry von Bülow, Walter's younger brother, northeast of Kemmel on this date while flying S.E.5a B.4890. Clark was wounded and became Harry von Bülow's fourth confirmed victory. Clark had 10 claims of his own at the time.

[64] There was no German Army Air Service uniform as such. Men wore the dress of their previous branch of service. Their new affiliation was however indicated by a small winged propeller device on each epaulet and, of course, if earned, they wore the appropriate flight qualification badge on their tunic.

Leutnant Walter von Bülow's debut as a fighter pilot began in *Feldflieger-Abteilung 22*. There, in 1915, he flew both the large twin-engine A.E.G. and the single-seater E-Type monoplane. In the photograph above von Bülow stands in front of A.E.G. G.II 19/15 and in the view below he is in the cockpit of a Fokker E.I that is being run up. But note the canvas cover on the barrel of the Spandau machine gun. After service in Palestine, von Bülow joined *Jagdstaffel 18* on the Western Front and then took over the leadership of *Jasta 36*. There he earned the *Orden Pour le Mérite* on October 8, 1917 with 21 victories to his credit. He added seven more before being named the Commanding Officer of *Jasta Boelcke* on December 12. With no further victories he was killed in air combat on January 6, 1918.

pilot might be in line for the Hohenzollern House Order had been adjusted upwards just as it had been for the *Orden Pour le Mérite*. It now usually took at least 10 victories before a man was considered worthy of a Hohenzollern and 20 was now generally needed for the even higher award. Requirements for these top Prussian awards had escalated along with the air war, a necessary precaution if they weren't to be cheapened by too widespread a distribution. Before von Bülow's recommendation for the Hohenzollern could be acted upon he shot down a Nieuport 12 on April 8 but on the same day that he was victorious over another F.E.2d, April 24, he was notified that the award was his. His final victory in *Jasta 18* came on May 7 when still one more F.E.2d became his victim.

Von Bülow was obviously displaying the qualities looked for in a squadron leader so when the *Staffelführer* of *Jasta 36* was wounded in a bombing raid on his unit's aerodrome, von Bülow was tapped for the job on May 15.[65] The next seven months were to show that his selection was a good one. As the new leader, his first success in his new command was a "double," just as it had been when he first joined *Jasta 18*. This time it was two observation balloons that he burned on May 20 in the vicinity of Bouvancourt. With him on the attack were two of his men who, together with von

Bülow, really wiped out the balloon line that day. According to squadron records, *Leutnant* Heinrich Bongartz got three of the balloons and *Leutnant* Theodor Quandt got two (the *Nachrichtenblatt* only credits Bongartz with two while confirming the others but dates the action as May 21, 1917, not May 20).[66]

The month of June 1917 was an inactive period for *Jasta 36* with no squadron victories being posted at all. It was the leader himself, von Bülow, who picked up the scoring again with successive victories on July 6 and 7. With a single victory in August and three in September he reached the 21 mark. His name was duly submitted for the *Pour le Mérite* which was approved on October 8. The honor brought with it no respite from the deadly business. Three more victories came later that month, one on the 18th and a "double" on the 24th, all Spads. Likewise, three more kills were recorded in November, on the 7th, the 23rd and the 29th, a Spad, a Sopwith single-seater and another Spad in that order. On December 2 he brought down a Bristol Fighter for his 28th, and as it turned out, last victory.

The famous *Jasta Boelcke* was now in need of a new leader. *Leutnant* Erwin Böhme, the man who had collided with Oswald Boelcke in mid-air on October 28, 1916 causing the latter's death, had

---

[65] The raid on *Jasta 36's* field took place on May 2, 1917. Shell splinters wounded the Commanding Officer, a highly decorated Badener from the Black Forest, *Leutnant* Albert Dossenbach, requiring his hospitalization. Dossenbach had received the Hohenzollern House Order and the *Pour le Mérite* in quick succession in von Bülow's old outfit, *Feldflieger-Abteilung 22*, the former coming on October 21 and the latter on November 11, 1916. His *Pour le Mérite* was in recognition of his eighth victory. That in itself was the norm in 1916, as we have seen. What made his award unusual was that all of Dossenbach's victories had been scored as a two-seater pilot. All of the other aviation *Pour le Mérites* up to then (there had been 11) had gone to men acting as fighter pilots. And there would be eight more awarded to fighter pilots after Dossenbach's before a flier acting in a different capacity received the high honor (this to a bomber squadron commander). Dossenbach's home state of Baden came through with its highest bravery award when he was given the Knight's Cross of the Military Karl-Friedrich Order on December 9 (this was the third aviation award of that exclusive order so far in the war and there would only be eight such awards in all).

Dossenbach's wound was not all that serious but he was given a temporary assignment at *Idflieg* for six weeks as he recovered. He was then given the command of *Jasta 10* on June 21, 1917. His overall score stood at 14 at this time and he raised this to 15 when he destroyed an observation balloon near Ypres in Flanders on June 27. On July 3, 1917 in a combat with four

British planes his gas tank was hit and Dossenbach either fell or jumped to his death from the burning aircraft.

[66] Bongartz had joined *Jasta 36* in April 1917 having served as a pilot in *Kasta 27* of *Kagohl 5* (he continued with the unit when it was converted into *Schusta 8*). In *Jasta 36* he was a consistent scorer and had raised his total to 24 confirmed victories when, finally, on November 24, 1917 he was recognized with the award of the Knight's Cross with Swords of the Royal Hohenzollern House Order. Bongartz was now equally eligible for the *Orden Pour le Mérite* and this came in short order. With his total raised to 27 by three more victories scored in the interim, he received that award personally from the *Kaiser* on December 23 in the field at a large review of the troops. Von Bülow attended the investiture. By then, Bongartz was the new commander of *Jasta 36* having taken over from von Bülow on December 13 when the latter was appointed the leader of *Jasta Boelcke*. Bongartz was three times wounded in *Jasta 36*. The first was a bullet in the arm during a combat on July 13, 1917. On March 30, 1918 he received a light head wound when hit by friendly flak. His third wounding put him out of action for good. On April 27, 1918, flying Fokker Triplane Dr.1 575/17, his left eye was shot away and although he was able to get down to a smooth landing, his combat days were over. His final victory tally was 33.

Quandt's two balloons on May 20, 1917 (or May 21) were his first two victories. He had come to *Jasta 36* after serving in *Flieger-Abteilung (A) 270*. Six more victories were racked up in *Jasta 36* in 1917, the last being on November 8. Quandt

gone down himself in flames on November 29, 1917.[67] With Bongartz's fine record there was an able person to take charge of *Jasta 36* and so von Bülow was given the command of *Jasta Boelcke* with effect from December 12. He had barely settled in when the former ex-hussar was shot down and killed on January 6 of the new year. Lt. W. M. Fry, a pilot in No. 23 Squadron, RFC who held the Military Cross, claimed a black Albatros D.V that day and von Bülow may well have been his ninth victory (out of a total claim of 11). However, pilots of another British squadron also claimed a D.V in the same general area of St. Julien/Passchendaele near Ypres that day. We may never know the final facts of von Bülow's death.

LEUTNANT PAUL SCHIRDEWAHN

Awarded the Knight's Cross of the Military St. Henry Order on October 27, 1917 when serving in *Flieger-Abteilung 28.*

Citation: "With the aviation detachment for over 1½ years, *Lt.* Schirdewahn flew over 100 enemy flights, in Macedonia, during the Romanian offensive, in the trench warfare in the east and in Dobrudscha under difficult conditions and against heavy resistance. His flight of over 500 kilometers from Braila to Odessa during which he took a number of essential photographs for the High Command under heavy flak fire was of major importance. This flight received praise in the Army Communique. Also praiseworthy was his leadership of an attack in squadron strength on Ismail. With cool nerve he flew at low level in the lead plane while other aircraft also made

excellent bomb runs so that the 835 kilograms of munitions resulted in a great success."

LEUTNANT HANS CLAUSEN

Awarded the Knight's Cross of the Military St. Henry Order on November 4, 1917 when serving in *Flieger-Abteilung (A)230.*

Citation: "After *Lt.* Clausen performed heroically as an observer, especially in the 1916 Battle of the Somme, he fought in the German 1917 summer offensive in East Galicia. There he distinguished himself by his coolness as an infantry cooperation flier. During a flight on July 21, he determined that one of our batteries was about to be attacked by the enemy. Despite poor ground conditions, he immediately landed and informed them of the situation. Then he took off again and through signal rockets he directed the battery's fire which allowed our infantry to advance. He was under infantry ground fire and defensive machine gun fire the entire time."

Hans Clausen's pre-air service unit was *Schützen-(Füsilier-)Regiment Prinz Georg Nr. 108* where he was serving at the outbreak of the war. Also in the unit before the war was *Leutnant* Ernst Clausen who, like Hans, earned the Knight's Cross of the Military St. Henry Order. The award to Ernst was made on June 4, 1917 and came for his performance as a machine gun company commander in the Aisne-Champagne battles. Ernst was born in Dresden on February 9, 1893 and Hans was born in the same city on April 9, 1894. It is

---

was appointed the Commanding Officer of *Jasta 53* on January 10, 1918 and received the Knight's Cross with Swords of the Royal Hohenzollern House Order on May 10 with his score still standing at eight. In fact, he was unable to gain a victory in *Jasta 53* before he was returned to *Jasta 36* on August 21 to take the *Staffelführer's* reigns from Harry von Bülow. There he was credited with victories nine through 15, with "doubles" on August 27 and September 3. His last came on the next day. In all, *Jasta 36* was officially credited with 120 aerial victories in the war.

[67] Böhme joined *Kasta 10* of *Kagohl 2* in December 1915 after being a pilot instructor at the flying school at Leipzig-Lindenthal. He was credited with a victory in *Kasta 10* and became one of the first group of pilots of the new *Jasta 2* which he joined on September 8, 1916. While he was old for a fighter pilot (he was age 37 at the time), he became a solid and consistent performer. On February 10, 1917 he scored his 12th confirmed victory. The next day, however, he was wounded in a combat with a Sopwith 1½ Strutter. While con-

valescing he was awarded the Knight's Cross with Swords of the Royal Hohenzollern House Order on March 12. When fit, he was named the *Staffelführer* of *Jasta 29* on July 2, getting a Nieuport there on July 14. On August 18 he returned to *Jasta 2* (now *Jasta Boelcke*) as its leader, replacing the ailing Otto Bernert. Due to casualties, the loss of a man like Voss to another unit and Walz's uninspired leadership, *Jasta Boelcke* had fallen on hard times. After Voss' departure, only two victories had been scored between May 20 and August 18 when Böhme came in. It wasn't long before he had the once proud unit back in form. In a little more than three months 30 confirmed victories were posted with Böhme himself accounting for 10 of them. Then on November 29, 1917 he scored his 24th victory when he downed a Sopwith Camel over Zonnebeke but fell in flames in a later attack on a two-seater. The proposal for his *Pour le Mérite* had been approved on November 24 and it is said that the badge arrived in the squadron mail just after Böhme had taken off on his last flight.

quite possible that they were brothers.

In the book *Sachsen in Grosser Zeit* ("Saxony in the Great Time") there are lists of recipients of the Military St. Henry Order and the two medals associated with it, the Gold and Silver St. Henry Medals, up to May 1917. In a list dated October 31, 1914 a *Leutnant* Clausen of the 108th Rifle Regiment is shown as receiving the Silver St. Henry Medal. Typical of such records, no first names are given. Since there were only two Lieutenants with that surname in the unit, it had to be either Hans or Ernst. What also is of passing interest is the fact that while St. Henry Medals had gone to junior officers in the War of 1870, by World War I they were meant for non-commissioned personnel only. But, obviously, early on in the war there was some carryover of this previous practice and in these lists, a few more *Leutnante* with Silver St. Henry Medals appear as late as 1915.

LEUTNANT FRITZ EINENCKEL

Awarded the Knight's Cross of the Military St. Henry Order on November 4, 1917 when serving in *Flieger-Abteilung (A)237*.

Citation: "In many more than 100 enemy flights, marked by bitter air battles, *Lt.* Einenckel, with no regard for his own well-being, through his results proved his ability and bravery. He especially distinguished himself as an infantry cooperation flier in the fierce battles on the "Winterberg" on the Chemin des Dames. In those days he never returned without machine gun hits to his aircraft but he always knew he had done his best for the beleaguered infantry."

Einenckel served in *Feldflieger-Abteilung 11* in the summer of 1916 and then was transferred to *Feldflieger-Abteilung 7* on September 6 of that year on what is believed to have been a temporary assignment. The date of his further transfer to *Flieger-Abteilung (A)237* is not known. In addition to his Knight's St. Henry, the roll shows that he held the Merit Order, Knight 2nd Class with Swords awarded to him in *Feldflieger-Abteilung 11* although with a date of January 18, 1917. He is known to have held the Albert Order, Knight 2nd Class with Swords as well as both Iron Crosses

and, rather strangely for a man born a native Saxon in Dresden, two awards from the Grand Duchy of Baden, its Merit Medal in Silver and the Knight 2nd Class with Swords of the Order of the Zähringer Lion.[68]

LEUTNANT JOHANNES KINZELMANN

Awarded the Knight's Cross of the Military St. Henry Order on November 11, 1917 when serving in *Jagdstaffel 7*.

Citation: "*Lt.* Kinzelmann frequently distinguished himself through his keenness and bravery as a single-seater fighter pilot in air battles. Among other things, he attacked an enemy squadron of Farmans by himself and caused one aircraft to crash in flames 8 kilometers behind the enemy lines. His propeller was shot up in the combat so it was only with extraordinary coolness that he was able to land behind German lines."

It is likely that the victory mentioned in the citation occurred on December 27, 1916 when Kinzelmann shot down a Farman near Louvemont around 11:00 a.m. German Time for his first, and so far as is known, only recorded victory. He had joined *Jasta 7* around October 13, 1916 as an *Offizier-Stellvertreter* after two-seater service with *Feldflieger-Abteilung 71* and *Artillerie-Flieger-Abteilung 208*. Shortly after arriving at *Jasta 7* he was promoted *Leutnant*.

Nothing further is known of Kinzelmann's service in *Jasta 7* nor what he might have done between his first victory and the award of the Knight's St. Henry 11 months later to merit that recognition. In the personal diary of the man who took over the leadership of *Jasta 7* in August 1917, Josef Jacobs, Kinzelmann rates just one mention. This was a flight he made with Jacobs on October 15, 1917 to make arrangements for some replacement aircraft at Ghent. What is strange is that Jacobs made no mention of Kinzelmann's high award even though Jacobs took a personal interest in such matters. For example, on November 10, 1917, just the day before Kinzelmann's St. Henry was approved, Jacobs noted the award of the Iron Cross, 1st Class to three of his men and remarked how pleased he was because these were the first

---

[68] Like Saxony, Baden tended to restrict its awards to natives, others serving in Baden contingents or to those who

rendered some particular service to the state. No such connection has been discovered in Einenckel's career.

Of the dozen men here, at least four served together in *Feldflieger-Abteilung 11* in 1915 and 1916. These were *Leutnant* Hellmuth von Schütz, seated on the coach at left, *Oberleutnant* Hermann Fricke, next to von Schütz with monocle, *Leutnant* Josef Jacobs, seated on the floor, and *Leutnant* Fritz Einenckel, standing at the right. The photograph can be dated between December 23, 1917 when Fricke received the *Pour le Mérite* (which he is wearing) and July 18, 1918 when Jacobs received his *Pour le Mérite* (which he is not wearing here). Einenckel received the Knight's Cross of the Military St. Henry Order in *Flieger-Abteilung (A)237* on November 4, 1917. Note he is wearing his cross in the buttonhole of his tunic. Also note the Hohenzollern Knight's Crosses with Swords worn by von Schütz and Jacobs. The unidentified man standing second from the left is also wearing the Knight 2nd Class with Swords of the Albert Order.

Three comrades in *Jasta 6* who, together, were credited with a total of 53 confirmed victories. Left to right: *Leutnant* Fritz Noltenius (20 victories), *Leutnant* Julius Schmidt (15 victories) and *Leutnant* Franz Hemer (18 victories). Schmidt was awarded the Knight's Cross of the Military St. Henry Order on November 11, 1917 while recovering from a serious wound received in combat on September 24 as a member of *Jasta 3*. He scored all his victories there but the wound ended his combat career. His later posting to *Jasta 6* was apparently in a non-combat capacity.

awards given out since he had taken charge of the unit. Kinzelmann was put at *Idflieg's* disposition on January 8, 1918 apparently for a transfer to *Jasta 55.* Then we lose track of him. Like so many others, there is much more to learn about Johannes Kinzelmann.

LEUTNANT JULIUS SCHMIDT

Awarded the Knight's Cross of the Military St. Henry Order on November 11, 1917 when serving in *Jagdstaffel 3.*

Citation: "As a member of *Jagdstaffel 3, Lt.* Schmidt was a standout in the air war and distinguished himself with skill and energy. Since April 1917, after he had already shot one aircraft down in *Kampfgeschwader IV,* he has shot down three aircraft in air combat with *Jagdstaffel 3.*"

Schmidt's citation understates his achievements in air combats by a considerable degree. By the time he was awarded his Knight's St. Henry on November 11, 1917, his confirmed victory score stood at 15. And he was already out of further aerial action for the rest of the war having suffered a serious wound in combat on September 24, 1917. The pace of his victories in the some five months in which he served in *Jasta 3* suggests that, had he not become a casualty, he could well have ended up as one of the top scoring German fighter pilots of the war. Of course, that could be said about many others on both sides whose promising careers were cut short by wounds, other injuries or death in action.

The date of Schmidt's first victory in a *Kampfgeschwader* is not recorded in any sources found so far. The first time his name appears in the *Nachrichtenblatt* is on May 19, 1917 when he is credited with his third victory, a Sopwith single-seater. Information on his second victory taken from squadron records is in some conflict. One set of data say that this occurred on April 28, 1917 with the destruction of an observation balloon. Another note has the victory on May 19 as his first. That latter statement is undoubtedly incorrect since the *Nachrichtenblatt* gives him credit for his fourth and fifth victories on May 25. They are listed there as an F.E. "Lattice Tail" and another Sopwith single-seater. Squadron records again contradict this. According to that source, a Sopwith

Pup was shot down by him on May 24, not May 25, but the other victory was on the following day and it was an F.E.2b. At any rate, it is evident that Schmidt closed out May of 1917 with five victories to his credit, all but one of which was scored in his short time with *Jasta 3.*

From here on, all sources are in agreement on the dates of Schmidt's remaining victories while not agreeing on the exact type of enemy aircraft in every instance. That is not surprising either since identifications were frequently mixed up by both the pilots themselves and the record keepers. There was only one definite action recorded for Schmidt in June, this being a Spad VII that was forced down. Apparently, it was not found in German lines since no official confirmation of it was given. On July 14 he scored twice, either two Martinsydes or a Martinsyde and a D.H.5, both confirmed. Another "double" was chalked up on July 28, this time reported by the *Nachrichtenblatt* as a Nieuport single-seater and a B.E. while squadron records mark them down as a Nieuport 17 and either a B.E.2 or a D.H.4. Victories over an R.E.8 on August 11 and a Sopwith Pup on August 12 were confirmed and in these instances, all sources were in agreement on the facts. A Sopwith Triplane was forced down on August 21 but no confirmation could be obtained. He closed out August with his 12th confirmed victory, a British fighter, probably a Sopwith Camel, shot down on the 22nd.

September 1917, Schmidt's last month in combat, saw his final three victories. On the 4th an R.E.8 went down, on the 9th a Nieuport scout was credited and the next day it was a Spad VII that was added to his score (squadron records say, however, that the plane was shot down on September 11, not September 10, the date listed in the *Nachrichtenblatt*). A combat on September 14 with either a Sopwith scout or an S.E.5 resulted in a claim but no confirmation. And then it was all over. In a fight with more British S.E.5s on September 24 Schmidt received his serious wound. A long period of recuperation ensued after which he reported to *Flieger-Ersatz-Abteilung 6,* the Saxon aviation replacement facility at Grossenhein. From there he was ordered to his first frontline posting in nearly a year. On September 9, 1918 he reported not to his old unit but, rather, to *Jasta 6* for assignment to non-combat duties where, presumably, he sat out the war.

The roll of the Merit Order lists Schmidt as

receiving the Knight 2nd Class with Swords of that award on December 1, 1916 but the unit given was not the *Kampfgeschwader 4* mentioned in his St. Henry citation but *Kampfstaffel 29* of *Kampfgeschwader 5*. A fine portrait photograph of Schmidt used on a postcard produced by the Berlin photographer W. Sanke and widely circulated for propaganda purposes throughout Germany along with many others of its war heroes tells us what his other awards were. Besides the Knight's St. Henry and the Merit Order Schmidt can be seen wearing ribbons indicative of the Albert Order, Knight 2nd Class with Swords, the Iron Cross, 2nd Class (he is also wearing the Iron Cross, 1st Class of course) and the Knight's Cross with Swords of the Royal Hohenzollern House Order.

OBERLEUTNANT KURT MESSOW

Awarded the Knight's Cross of the Military St. Henry Order on November 21, 1917 when serving in *Schutzstaffel 8* with *Flieger-Abteilung (A)216*.

Citation: "As a reconnaissance and battle flier in the campaigns on the Somme, the Aisne and at Verdun, *Oblt.* Messow, through example a model of bravery, attained achievements that put him on the top of his section. On October 19, 1917, in the 7th Army sector near Laon, he attacked repeatedly showing exemplary nerve. With his section and at low altitude and with outstanding results they dropped over 100 kilograms of bombs on a battery that was firing furiously and expended about 3,000 machine gun rounds at concentrations of assault troops."

LEUTNANT PAUL ERBGUTH

Awarded the Knight's Cross of the Military St. Henry Order on December 2, 1917 when serving in *Jagdstaffel 30*.

Citation: "After *Lt.* Erbguth was seriously wounded in the leg on April 30, 1915 with Territorial Reserve Infantry Regiment 107, he joined the air service when barely healed. A member since April 23, 1916, he proved himself to be a brave and competent pilot in many air battles. On September 21, 1917, he shot down his second enemy plane behind our lines."

Erbguth came to *Jasta 30* after service in *Schusta 21*. His first victory was scored on April 26, 1917

when he was credited with a B.E.2d in *Jasta 30*. The September 21 victory was over a Sopwith Camel. On December 28, 1917 he was appointed the Commanding Officer of *Jasta 54,* a Saxon formation. For reasons unknown, he was replaced in that post on May 18, 1918. The rest of Erbguth's wartime service is likewise unknown.

OBERLEUTNANT MAX HERRMANN-MILLINGTON

Awarded the Knight's Cross of the Military St. Henry Order on December 2, 1917 when serving in *Flieger-Abteilung (A)264*.

Citation: "*Oblt.* Herrmann-Millington, seriously wounded in October 1914 fighting with Lancer Regiment 21, volunteered for the air service after his recovery. From October 1915 on, together with his brother as a crew member, later fallen in air battle, he distinguished himself in the highest manner by his bravery as part of *Geschwader 2* of the Army High Command. In concert with *Kampfstaffel 11* on August 19, 1916 he attacked a Russian troop encampment east of Toboly on the Stochod with bombs and machine gun fire. Thereby a Russian cavalry division, poised to break through at Rutka-Szerwiszcze by crossing the Stochod, was discovered. The *Kampfstaffel* attacked the horsemen with machine gun fire and sent them scattering in all directions. Through his daring flying *Oblt.* Herrmann-Millington distinguished himself as he also did in a bombing attack at Luck on September 2, 1916 when he was attacked by two enemy aircraft. He forced one plane down and turned back the other.

At the end of January 1917, *Oblt.* Herrmann-Millington took part in the bombing of the industrial area of Nancy with great distinction. His health was weakened by many hours of flying in the cold and upon landing, he had to be carried from his aircraft."

HIS ROYAL HIGHNESS *RITTMEISTER PRINZ* FRIEDRICH SIGISMUND OF PRUSSIA

Awarded the Knight's Cross of the Military St. Henry Order on December 3, 1917 when serving in *Flieger-Abteilung 22*.

Citation: "In the trench warfare between (Lake)

The pilots of *Jagdstaffel 30* line up for the photographer on a chilly late 1917 day with their Albatros fighters as a backdrop. Eighth from the left is the Commanding Officer, the 20-victory ace who was killed in action on March 17, 1918, *Oberleutnant* Hans Bethge. Second from the right is *Leutnant* Paul Erbguth who was awarded the St. Henry Order Knight's Cross on December 2, 1917, shortly before he left *Jasta 30* to assume the command of *Jasta 54*.

Two, possibly three, St. Henry Order winners are in this photograph of *Flieger-Abteilung (A)264* at *Schloss* Roucourt in the early summer of 1917. The Commanding Officer, *Hauptmann* Paul Sommer, with hands folded on first step, received the Knight's Cross of the order on May 3, 1917 when in *Kampfgeschwader 2*. On his left is *Oberleutnant* Max Herrmann-Millington who would win the Knight's Cross with *(A)264* on December 2, 1917. The man on Sommer's right is identified as an *Oberleutnant* Rössler. He could be the Kurt Roesler who earned the Knight's St. Henry Order on November 17, 1916 in *Feldflieger-Abteilung 24, Fl.Abt. (A)264's* earlier designation.

Rittmeister Prinz Friedrich Sigismund of Prussia was awarded the Knight's Cross of the Military St. Henry Order on December 3, 1917 for operations on the Eastern Front that summer and fall. All princes of Prussia received the highest grades of the main Prussian orders upon attaining their 10th year. This included the Grand Commander of the Royal Hohenzollern House Order which was worn from a collar chain. The Prince is wearing that badge with Swords at the neck in this photograph in the manner a Commander's badge would be worn. Swords were added to his insignia in World War I not so much for outright bravery but simply to recognize the wartime service by a man of his high station.

In the photograph below, the Prince, who was a qualified pilot, stands in front of the nose of an L.V.G. B.I wearing the service cap of his pre-war unit, *2. Leib-Husaren-Regiment Königin Victoria von Preussen Nr. 2,* another of these units using the famous "death's head" skull and crossbones insignia. The photo was taken at *Feldflieger-Abteilung 46* on the Russian Front in April 1915.

Narocz and (Lake) Dryswjaty near Dünaburg, Jacobstadt and Riga, *Rittmeister Prinz* Friedrich Sigismund of Prussia distinguished himself as a pilot through his bravery and nerve from May 25 to August 31, 1917. During the storming of the bridgehead at Jacobstadt between September 21 and 22, 1917, the 8th Army High Command entrusted the leadership of all the flying units involved to him, the success of which was praised in the Army Communique of September 22, mentioning especially the Prince."

It is not clear from this whether the Prince was actually at risk in the September 21 and 22, 1917 operation or whether he merely coordinated the aerial support from the ground. There was another "flying Prince of Prussia," however, who flew operationally and paid the price for it. He was *Rittmeister Prinz* Friedrich Karl who was the Deputy Leader of *Flieger-Abteilung (A)258.* At every opportunity, though, he went up as a fighter pilot as a volunteer. On March 21, 1917, flying an old Albatros D.I from the adjacent *Jasta Boelcke,* his plane was crippled and he was brought down in No-Man's Land. In attempting to scramble back to the German lines he was shot by Australian infantry and captured. He died of his wounds in an English hospital on April 7, 1917 (some records say April 6, 1917).

LEUTNANT HANS DONATH

Awarded the Knight's Cross of the Military St. Henry Order on January 7, 1918 when serving in *Flieger-Abteilung (A)213.*

Citation: "On September 5, 1917, *Lt.* Donath, who had already flown over 150 enemy flights, his aircraft damaged 18 times in air battles, led a reconnaissance flight over the enemy hinterlands. Attacked by three fighter planes, he broke away from the first and, in attacking the second, his pilot was hit in the shoulder. Coolly, *Lt.* Donath turned the pursuing attacker away, covered the wounded pilot and enabled him to return to an airfield behind their lines. On November 10, 1917 he flew at 200 meters over enemy positions and right through the artillery registration area. Despite heavy defensive fire and a damaged aircraft, he determined the status of their advance and the strength of their positions. He did not turn back until the recon-

naissance was finished."

LEUTNANT LOTHAR NAGEL

Awarded the Knight's Cross of the Military St. Henry Order on January 26, 1918 when serving in *I. Marine-Küsten-Flieger-Abteilung.*

Citation: "With the *I. Marine-Küsten-Flieg.-Abt.* since January 1917, *Lt.* Nagel flew more than 100 enemy flights as an artillery observer. Despite heavy opposition, he was fearless in his duties and directed firing at heavy batteries and long range targets. Among the many air battles in which he engaged, he shot down one of several aircraft that attacked him in September 1917. A special achievement of his was the fact that although he was forced to make emergency landings twice in one day, he immediately took off again for the next shoot."

A victory for *Leutnant* Nagel is not listed in the *Nachrichtenblatt* for September 1917 but only a few of them scored by the German naval airmen appear there anyway. Nagel died in Cologne on October 4, 1918 in unknown circumstances.

OBERLEUTNANT HERMANN MARTINI

Awarded the Knight's Cross of the Military St. Henry Order on February 6, 1918 when serving in *Jagdstaffel 12.*

Citation: "Since July 1915, *Oblt.* Martini has been a member of the air service, initially as an observer. After the stand against the Brusilov Offensive in the summer of 1916 and the campaign against Romania in 1917, he went for flight training to become a fighter pilot. In that capacity he has been a member of *Jagdstaffel 12* since November. On his first such flight during the Battle of Cambrai, together with some comrades he forced an English aircraft down after a hard battle over Bourlon Wood. On November 30, during the German counterattack at Cambrai, he shot down an English fighter pilot. It is a very special achievement that despite enemy resistance and bad weather, *Oblt.* Martini fought two victorious air battles at the very beginning of his career as a fighter pilot."

Martini had earlier served in *Feldflieger-*

According to the citation for his Knight's Cross of the Military Order of St. Henry which he received on February 6, 1918, *Oberleutnant* Hermann Martini, shown here with an Albatros D.Va, earned it for two victories the previous November while with *Jagdstaffel 12*. But the photograph below shows a celebration in *Jasta 58,* which Martini commanded in 1918, for the award of an *Ehrenbecher* to him. It usually took only three or four weeks after a man's first victory before the cup actually arrived. Here Martini clutches the champagne bottle being thrust at him while *Leutnant* Martin Dehmisch, the unit's star performer with 10 victories, holds Martini's *Ehrenbecher* and a fistful of cigars.

Abteilung 36 where the roll shows him receiving the Merit Order, Knight 2nd Class with Swords on December 1, 1916. No evidence can be found that the two victories credited to him in *Jasta 12* were ever officially confirmed. The War Diary of *Jasta 12* does not record any victories at all in November 1917 (the Battle of Cambrai began on November 20, 1917 with a surprise British attack but the German counterattack regained all the ground that had been won; a great opportunity was lost mainly because the British had no plan to exploit their initial successes). Further, Martini's name does not appear anywhere in the unit's records. Most certainly, he was not in *Jasta 12* at the time of his award of the Knight's St. Henry. On January 28, 1918 he took over the command of the newly formed *Jasta 58.* He remained its leader until the end of the war, with time out for shuttling between assignments with *Jagdgruppe 3* and *Armee-Flug-Park 2.*

The accompanying undated photograph shows the party at *Jasta 58* celebrating the award of the *Ehrenbecher* to Martini. Since it usually took no more than three or four weeks for an *Ehrenbecher* to catch up with a man by late 1917 or early 1918, this strongly suggests that Martini's first official victory was scored in *Jasta 58.* Of interest in terms of further successes he may have had is a proposal dated October 10, 1918 found in the Bavarian *Kriegsarchiv* in Munich. In this document, four fighter pilots, all Commanding Officers of *Jasta* then comprising *Jagdgruppe 7,* were proposed for the award of the Bavarian Military Merit Order, 4th Class with Swords. The four were *Leutnant* Emil Thuy of *Jasta 28, Leutnant* Carl-August von Schoenebeck of *Jasta 33, Leutnant* Paul Strähle of *Jasta 57* and Martini of *Jasta 58.*[70] In Martini's proposal it was stated that his command had accounted for 10 enemy planes and four observation balloons in the period August 24 to September 16, 1918. However, none was specifically credited to Martini himself, something that would usually be mentioned if, in fact, he had accounted for any of these victories. It is of passing interest to note that for some reason, perhaps the fact that the war ended before any action was taken, that none of the men ever received the award.

Martini served in the post-war *Reichswehr* and was promoted *Rittmeister* on June 1, 1922. In addition to his Knight's St. Henry and the Merit Order, the *Ranglisten* during that period show that he also held the Albert Order, Knight 2nd Class with Swords, both Iron Crosses and the Military Merit Cross, 3rd Class with War Decoration from the Austro-Hungarian Empire.

LEUTNANT ERICH VON NEINDORFF

Awarded the Knight's Cross of the Military St. Henry Order on February 9, 1918 when serving in *Flieger-Abteilung (A)284.*

Citation: "With the aviation detachment since the end of February 1917, *Lt.* von Neindorff proved himself a brave and capable flier in over 80 enemy flights. On June 15, he and his observer flew a strategic mission of 400 kilometers, from Sundau to the Champagne behind the enemy lines. This flight, up to that time, was the longest straight line flight over enemy territory. This dashing and unusually energetic flight brought valuable information for the Army leadership. In the battles before Verdun in July 1917 he also distinguished himself as an infantry and artillery cooperation flier."

More details of the June 15 flight were contained in a mention published in the *Nachrichtenblatt* of June 21, 1917. It read:

"Strategic Reconnaissance:

An aircraft of *Fliegerabteilung A284,* pilot *Leutnant* v. Neindorff, observer *Lt.* Deetjen, took off on 15.6. at 7:15 a.m. from the airfield at Ruestenhard, southwest of Neu-Breisach (*A.A. B.*), flew over Belfort, Vesoul, Jussey, Langres, Joinville en Ballage, Vitry le Francois, and landed after a flight of 460 km. at Bouziers (3rd Army) at 10:45 a.m.[71]

The aircraft returned the same day to its home field. For the reconnaissance results, look under the Activities of the Air Force on 15.6."

Then under "Special Accomplishments" we have

---

[70] Thuy ended the war with 32 confirmed victories, von Schoenebeck with eight and Strähle with 14. All three received the Knight's Cross with Swords of the Royal Hohenzollern House Order and Thuy was awarded the *Orden Pour le Mérite* (on June 30, 1918 when his score stood at 23).
[71] *A.A. B* stood for (Headquarters) *Armee-Abteilung B.*

A D.F.W. C.V forms the backdrop to this photograph taken on the airfield of *Jasta 43*. *Leutnant* Otto Creutzmann, second from the right, earned the Knight's Cross of the Military St. Henry Order in this unit. However, by the time it was approved, July 19, 1918, Creutzmann had been appointed Commanding Officer of *Jasta 46*. He scored seven victories in all, one in *Jasta 20* in 1917, three in *Jasta 43* and his final three in *Jasta 46,* these last six all occurring between April and August of 1918. The men here are, left to right: *Leutnant* Haake, Unknown, Creutzmann and *Leutnant* Dehne.

The group of well turned out airmen from *Brieftauben-Abteilung-Ostende* on a stroll in the seaside town of Ostend, Belgium in October 1915 includes *Oberleutnant* (then *Leutnant*) Karl Persch, at the extreme left. Persch was killed on a mission with *Bosta 7* of *Bogohl 6* on August 25, 1918. His award of the Knight's Cross of the Military St. Henry Order was approved on September 1, another of the relatively few posthumous awards that were made of this order. The men here are, left to right, Persch, *Lt.* von Carlowitz, *Lt.* von Wittenhorst, *Lt.* Rössing, *Rittm.* Marx, *Lt.* Lochte and *Hptm.* Böhmer.

Creutzmann's citation for his Knight's St. Henry credited him with four victories through May 1918 so the unconfirmed claim of March 24 must have been counted in arriving at this figure). Creutzmann replaced *Oberleutnant* Josef Loeser who had been killed on June 3.[75.]

In *Jasta 46* Creutzmann scored three more victories, all S.E.5as, to bring his tally up to seven by war's end. These were a twin victory on August 8 and the final one on August 10.

LEUTNANT WALTER HEINE

Awarded the Knight's Cross of the Military St. Henry Order on July 19, 1918 when serving in *Flieger-Abteilung (A)276*.

Citation: "With *Flieg.-Abt. 276* since August 1917, *Lt.* Heine so distinguished himself on his many enemy flights that he was highly praised by the detachment commander. The many written and verbal recognitions the detachment received from the Army High Command were, according to the detachment commander's statement, thanks to the excellent work of this Saxon officer. Especially noteworthy, aside from *Lt.* Heine's bravery and tenacity, is his tactical understanding that made his reports more valuable to the Army High Command. *Lt.* Heine was previously recognized with the Silver St. Henry Medal in May 1916."

Heine is the first of two Knight's St. Henry aviation recipients who are known to have received the Silver St. Henry Medal earlier. There was a third man who might also have earned both awards (see Page 128). Heine's medal was earned when he was a *Vizefeldwebel* in *Feldartillerie-Regiment Nr. 192.* Shortly thereafter he was promoted *Offizier-Stellvertreter* and then *Leutnant* in the same unit. His award of the Silver St. Henry Medal was carried in

Sachsen in grosser Zeit on a list dated August 3, 1916. As noted earlier in connection with these lists, the actual award date was some weeks earlier.

LEUTNANT GERHARD HEYM

Awarded the Knight's Cross of the Military St. Henry Order on July 19, 1918 when serving in *Flieger-Abteilung (A)233.*

Citation: During the 1918 spring German advance in Russia, *Lt.* Heym had several daring achievements in the air. On February 18 he thwarted the escape of enemy aircraft from the Russian aerodrome at Dünaburg and caused severe damage by destroying railway equipment 100 kilometers behind enemy lines. On April 29, from a height of only 50 meters, he determined the location of the enemy lines despite strong ground defences and made important reports to the High Command. On May 7, in a severe air battle in which he managed to escape only by the complete mastery of his machine, both he and his observer were seriously wounded. The machine took 50 hits. Thanks to his spirit and resolve, he was able to reach his own aerodrome 15 kilometers away."

OBERLEUTNANT KARL PERSCH

Awarded the Knight's Cross of the Military St. Henry Order on September 1, 1918 when serving in *Bombenstaffel 7* of *Bombengeschwader 6.*

Citation: "*Oblt.* Persch, through his personal example as a flight leader, led his men in such a manner that the unit was the first in the number of missions completed, the number of bombs dropped and in other measureable results. They alone, on the nights of July 12, 13, 15 and 16,

---

[75.] Loeser had begun fighter pilot training at *Jastaschule I* on November 13, 1917 after service in *Feldflieger-Abteilung 40/Flieger-Abteilung 40.* After a few days of familiarization at *Jasta 1,* he was named the Commanding Officer of *Jasta 39* on December 4 and served with that unit on the Italian Front for two months. His first victory was scored there on January 11, 1918, a Sopwith Camel, and he got his second on February 4, another Sopwith. In that latter combat he was wounded and had to be relieved. When he was fit again, he assumed the command of *Jasta 46* on the Western Front on April 23. He scored no confirmed victories while in that job and met his death on June 3 when he and one of his men made a deter-

mined attack on first one and then two R.E.8s of No. 3 Squadron, Australian Flying Corps, over Hamel. The pair had made two passes at the crew of Lt. T.L. Baillieu, D.F.C. (pilot) and Lt. F.A. Sewell (observer) when their R.E.8 was joined by the other one crewed by Lt. H.C. Armstrong (pilot) and Lt. J.H. Jeffery (observer). Loeser was in the lead on this third attack and came under the combined fire of the two Australian observers. His Albatros fell and burst into flames upon impact in Vaire Wood. Loeser's wingmate attempted another attack on Baillieu and Sewell but with no result and broke off.

The fourth ribbon on the *Feldschnalle* of the 19-victory *Pour le Mérite* ace, *Leutnant* Kurt Wintgens, is his Albert Order, Knight 2nd Class with Swords which he received on July 19, 1916 for his performance in *Feld-flieger-Abteilung 67*. He is shown above with the wreckage of Morane Biplane No. 5177 which he shot down on August 2, 1916. The crew of Lt. J.A.N. Ormsby and 2/Lt. H.J. Newton of No. 60 Squadron, RFC were both killed. Below he is seen in the cockpit of a Halberstadt D.II. Wintgens was killed in a combat on September 25, 1916 as a member of the newly formed *Jasta 1*. His aircraft disintegrated in the air, apparently hit in the fuel tank by explosive bullets.

Of the total of only eight *Pour le Mérites* going to German observers, the last three, including one to *Oberleutnant* Albert Müller-Kahle, left, were awarded on October 13, 1918. Müller-Kahle was also a recipient of the Albert Order, Knight 2nd Class with Swords. Shown with him here is his pilot, *Vizefeldwebel* Ernst Nitschmann, wearing the non-commissioned officer's counterpart award to the *Pour le Mérite,* the Golden Military Merit Cross, in his buttonhole. Both served in *Flieger-Abteilung 6* where Nitschmann received his high award on July 16, 1918.

Leutnant Friedrich Nielebock was the fourth observer to earn the *Orden Pour le Mérite* when he received it in *Flieger-Abteilung (A)250* on June 2, 1918. *Fl. Abt. (A)250* was a Saxon formation and this accounted for his receiving the Albert Order, Knight 2nd Class with Swords. In the proposal for his *Pour le Mérite* Nielebock's Commanding Officer cited his 280 frontline flights in the 18 months he had served as an observer in Flanders successfully calling in counter-battery fire on more than 1,000 enemy artillery positions and other important ground targets.

Here we have four holders of the Albert Order, Knight 2nd Class with Swords, all of whom served in *Feldflieger-Abteilung 23* and three of whom were fated not to survive the war.

Leutnant Helmuth le Blanc, Knight's Cross on December 1, 1916, died in hospital on March 3, 1917.

The Military St. Henry recipient, *Oberleutnant* Willy Meyer, Knight's Cross on July 15, 1915.

Leutnant Walter Sieber, Knight's Cross on June 8, 1916, killed in action on July 15, 1916 with the St. Henry winner, *Oberleutnant* Jakob von Hartsen.

Leutnant Erwin Tütschulte, Knight's Cross on June 8, 1916, killed in action on June 25, 1916 as a Fokker pilot with *FF1.Abt. 23*.

A trio of ribbons adorn the tunic of the later *Luftwaffe* paratroop general, *Oberleutnant* Kurt Student, here posing when he was the leader of *Jasta 9*. The top ribbon carries the crowned crossed swords device indicative of his Knight's Cross with Swords of the Hohenzollern House Order. Next is the ribbon of the Iron Cross, 2nd Class. Finally, we have the ribbon of his Albert Order with just plain crossed swords. He received the Knight 2nd Class with Swords on June 15, 1915 when serving with *Feldflieger-Abteilung 17*. A pre-war flier, Student earned his Pilot's Badge in 1913.

Student (marked by an "X") is greeted by fellow officers, ground crew and his mascot (marked by an "XX") after a mission with his *Eindecker*. After his two-seater service, Student became a member of the *Fokkerstaffel* of the 3rd Army and then assumed the command of *Jasta 9* upon its mobilization in October 1916. Student relinquished that command on March 5, 1918 after scoring five victories. The arm patch on the left sleeve of the observer with hand on hip identifies him as having served in *Feldflieger-Abteilung 22*.

whether a single St. Henry ribbon denoted the Silver or the Gold (or the Knight's Cross of the order for that matter). This confusion could not have existed in the case of the only man to receive, progressively, the Silver St. Henry Medal, the Gold St. Henry Medal and the Knight's Cross of the order. He was *Leutnant* Richard Walter Kühn of 5. *Infanterie-Regiment Kronprinz Nr. 104.* The three St. Henry ribbons that he was entitled to wear could only mean both medals and the Knight's Cross. Sadly, this intrepid company commander received his eighth and fatal wound on October 15, 1918 and was taken prisoner of war by the British. Three days later Kühn died of his injuries.

— There were at least 22 Silver St. Henry Medal-only recipients who earned their awards in the ground troops and then won the Knight's Cross of the order after they were commissioned officers. As already covered, two and possibly three of these men later transferred to the *Fliegertruppe* where they earned the order.

award there had already been 114 bestowals of the high honor within the ground troops so this was a considerable breakthrough for the air service. What had it taken to get such signal recognition? Fortunately, Sattler himself recorded an action that almost surely was the thing that persuaded the authorities to act. It was a volunteer night reconnaissance mission in Romania to ascertain whether the opposing Russian forces were massing for an attack. Sattler does not mention the date but a study of the maps and text in the German and Austrian official histories by a knowledgeable historian in this country indicate that the date would have been around Christmas, 1916, one or two days either side. This ties in perfectly with the approval of his award two months later.

On the date in question, the weather all day had been stormy and totally unfit for flying. That evening the air crews were gathered in *(A)278's* mess when the Commanding Officer was summoned to the phone to receive an urgent message from the German 9th Army Headquarters. The

GOLD ST. HENRY MEDAL AVIATION RECIPIENTS

The three airmen who had the distinction of receiving the Gold St. Henry Medal were:

Rank at Time of Award and Name of Recipient	Unit in Which Recipient Served at Time of Award	Date of Award
Offz.-Stv. Rudolf Sattler	*Flieger-Abteilung (A)278*	February 28, 1917
Offz.-Stv. Paul Aue	*Jagdstaffel 10*	July 24, 1917
Vzfw. Walter Dittrich	*Jagdstaffel 1*	July 24, 1917

OFFIZIER-STELLVERTRETER RUDOLF SATTLER

Awarded the Gold St. Henry Medal on February 28, 1917 when serving in *Flieger-Abteilung (A)278.*

Citation: "With daring nerve and skillful flying he went forward into battle against superior opponents."

The economic language employed in Sattler's citation tells us virtually nothing about the deed or deeds that warranted the first aviation award of the Gold St. Henry Medal. Up to the date of his

High Command needed confirmation of a statement made by a Russian deserter that an attack was coming. Ordinarily, something like this might not be taken too seriously but a spy for the Germans had also brought in the same intelligence. If an assault were in the offing, it would require swift redeployment of German troops and the matter could not await daylight. Besides, it was felt an aerial reconnaissance, even at night, would be more effective than ground patrols since the German infantry was exhausted from the rigors of their recent advance.

The plan was to send out one aircraft and have it fly over the Russian lines and by counting the number of enemy camp fires and their locations,

Offizier-Stellvertreter Rudolf Sattler, here in post-war uniform, was the first of only three airmen in World War I to receive the Gold St. Henry Medal. It was awarded on February 28, 1917 when he was a pilot in *Flieger-Abteilung (A)278.* Earlier, in *(A)278's* predecessor unit, *Feldflieger-Abteilung 29,* he, like the other two aviation Gold Medal recipients, had first earned the Silver St. Henry Medal. Sattler's Silver award appeared on a list dated March 7, 1916.

From the unofficial pins adorning the crown of his service cap, it would appear that this photograph of *Offizier-Stellvertreter* Paul Aue was also taken after the war when such liberties could be taken. He is wearing his Gold St. Henry Medal which was awarded on July 24, 1917 (although Aue himself dates it more than a year later; see text for details), his Silver St. Henry Medal which was announced on a list dated April 6, 1917 and his Silver Friedrich August Medal. Both St. Henry Medals came for his service in *Jasta 10* where he was credited with nine official victories. His total score was 10. He had scored his first victory as a two-seater pilot in *Kagohl 5* in October 1916.

get an estimate of the enemy's strength, which of his forces were in position and what his intentions seemed to be. If this plane did not return in three hours, a second would be dispatched with the same objective. If this one, too, did not get back, then a third was to be ready to go. At that time no provisions had been made for night flights on this front. There was not even so much as a pocket lantern for emergency signaling. So this was strictly a volunteer mission and Sattler and his unnamed observer were the first to step forward and were ordered to take the first aircraft out. Just before the car that was to drive the crew to the field arrived, Sattler added a few lines to what was called "the last letter", the one many fliers had prepared to be sent home in the event they failed to return from a mission.

Permission had been given to light two bonfires to point them in the general direction they were to take because there was a solid deck of low clouds. In the darkness Sattler could not read any of his instruments including the altimeter and compass. It was nearly blind flying. They knew that the Transylvanian alp they had to cross, Mont Odobesti, was over 3,000 feet high. They picked up the signal fires and began their climb. The mountainous terrain generated strong crosswinds and navigating was extremely difficult in the rough air. They negotiated Mont Odobesti successfully and crossed the front lines. At this point Sattler's observer ordered him to drop down so that they could begin their reconnaissance. As the observer began to search for the telltale camp fires, Sattler had to fly lower and lower if anything were going to be picked out. His left hand was always on the throttle in case he had to apply emergency power suddenly if they got too close to the ground. Sattler could not read his gas gauge either and apparently they had failed to keep careful track of the duration of their flight so now they began to fear that they might run out of fuel. A forced landing in the hilly country below would surely mean, as Sattler put it, "broken necks and arms." Fortunately, they encountered no ground fire at all.

They then moved on and found another landmark, the Putna River. Behind it they spotted a few camp fires and attracted a bit of flak. But nowhere did they see the scale of activity that would have suggested an enemy counterattack was in the making. This satisfied the crew that they had fulfilled their mission and in skies that were mercifully clearing a bit, they set a course for home. Once again they cleared Mont Odobesti and

picked up the friendly directional fires that were still burning. The road that ran alongside their airfield between Focsani and Ploesti could now be easily picked out and then they saw that the field itself was ringed with torches. Their Commanding Officer had taken this added precaution in helping to get them down safely because the field was narrow and poorly situated.

Now came the tricky business of a night landing, something Sattler had never attempted before. Again his left hand was on the throttle in case a surge of power was required. Both unstrapped themselves and his observer leaned far out of his cockpit and over the side to pick up the ground as they glided down. Just as they were about to touch down, Sattler's comrade shouted, "Gas! Gas! We are going into the trees!" Sattler opened the throttle, the plane rose up and over the trees and settled to a soft landing at the far end of the field, as good as any in daylight. The C.O. and the entire squadron had been on the field just about ready to bid the back-up aircraft farewell. Sattler and his observer had been aloft for nearly three hours and hope for their safe return with the needed intelligence had been fading. A call was immediately placed to 9th Army Headquarters with the welcome information that there was absolutely no evidence of an enemy buildup for an imminent offensive. Later that same night a *Herr* von Falkenhain" called the *Kasino* and interrupted the celebration going on at *(A)278* to offer his personal congratulations on the first successful night mission of an aircraft attached to the 9th Army.

The next morning what must have been a very tired crew repeated the same flight made only a few hours before. This time Sattler's observer was able to take numerous photographs of the ground they had covered in darkness. The results proved their original reconnaissance had been accurate. There were no indications of an impending enemy attack. Sattler concluded his story with the wry remark, "How much easier it (the daylight flight) was than in the darkness."

As a *Vizefeldwebel* Sattler had received the Silver St. Henry Medal in the predecessor unit of *(A)278, Feldflieger-Abteilung 29*. The date recorded in *Sachsen in grosser Zeit* is March 7, 1916, only the third aviation recipient up to that time (see Appendix XIV). He ended his wartime service in *Flieger-Ersatz-Abteilung 5* at Hannover. After the Armistice, Sattler stayed in the service but with aviation prohibited by the Treaty of Versailles, he reverted to the infantry and was promoted *Leutnant* in 1922. Sattler received two of Saxony's lesser bravery awards for non-comissioned officers and men, the Honor Cross with Swords and the Friedrich August Medal in Silver, both, presumably, before the award of his St. Henry medals (these lesser awards will be covered in the next two chapters). He also held the Saxon Service Decoration, 1st Class (for 15 years service), a Bravery Medal (class unknown) from the Austro-Hungarian Empire, the Wound Badge in Black and, as would be expected, the Iron Cross in both 1st and 2nd Class.

OFFIZIER-STELLVERTRETER PAUL AUE

Awarded the Gold St. Henry Medal on July 24, 1917 when serving in *Jagdstaffel 10*.

Citation: "Aue brought down four enemy aircraft in a short period of time, all confirmed by the Commanding General of the Air Force. His extraordinary commitment and nerve deserve special recognition."

Once again, we are fortunate in being able to add details to the bare bones of the citation itself. The four victories mentioned were all scored between March 25 and June 7, 1917 when Aue was a fighter pilot with *Jasta 10*. Not mentioned is the fact that he joined *Jasta 10* with one victory already to his credit. This was scored when he was flying with *Kampfstaffel 30* of *Kampfgeschwader 5*. On October 25, 1916 he and his observer, a *Leutnant* Fäth, shot down a British B.E. for a confirmed victory.

Aue's first victory in *Jasta 10* came on March 25, 1917 when he got a Nieuport. He was a *Vizefeldwebel* at the time. This event could well have triggered his award of the Silver St. Henry Medal because the announcement of his receiving it is carried in *Sachsen in grosser Zeit* on a list dated April 6, 1917. The dates of his third and fourth vic-

tories have not been found but are known to have been confirmed prior to June 7, 1917 when he scored again, this time his victim being a Spad scout. In between, he put in for two more claims, both of which were awarded to other German pilots. The first of these was a dispute about who should get the credit for a Sopwith Triplane that went down on May 23. In the event it was given to *Leutnant* Hans Hinsch (or Hintsch) of *Jasta 11*.[7] Aue lost out again on May 27 when an S.E.5 was counter-claimed by another German pilot who was awarded the victory.[8] The end of June 1917 saw *Jasta 10* being amalgamated with *Jasta 4, 6* and *11* to form the first permanent grouping of fighters of true squadron strength, *Jagdgeschwader Nr. 1*. The purpose of the new formation, and the other three that were ultimately formed, was to achieve aerial superiority over particularly critical areas of an Army front. Thus the four flights of a *Jagdgeschwader* could always be expected to be in the thick of things, where air fighting was at its hottest. Even so, Aue was unable to add to his score all through the rest of June and all of July and August. September proved to be a dry period as well until the 19th when he was wounded in a combat with British planes in the Roulers area (possibly Spads of No. 19 Squadron, RFC).

Aue himself claimed that he continued on active operations for nearly a year before he was forced to seek hospital treatment (see his own account later on). If he did, it was again without further success until well into the new year when he brought down a Bristol F2b "Fighter" for his sixth confirmed victory on May 3, 1918. There is some confusion about what was marked down as his seventh victory. The *Nachrichtenblatt* credits him with an observation balloon destroyed on June 16. Aue remembered his opponent that day as quite a different target (again, see his account). A pair of Sopwith Camels were recorded in August, one on the 19th and the other on the 29th. His tenth, and last, victory was scored on October 4 when he was credited with a Spad.

---

[7] This was Hinsch's third confirmed victory. Only two days later he was dead. Some data suggest he was shot down on May 24 in an air combat which would have meant he died of wounds the following day.

[8] The *Nachrichtenblatt* credits two *Jasta 33* pilots with S.E.5s on May 27, 1917, *Leutnant* Johann Hesselink and *Offizier-Stellvertreter* Martin Altmaier. The *Jasta 33* War Diary confirms these victories but states that only one of the aircraft was an S.E.5. Altmaier's claim is listed as S.E.5 A.8905 which was flown by 2/Lt. E.A. Floyd of No. 56

Squadron, RFC who was made a prisoner (No. 56 Squadron was the first squadron to receive the S.E.5 and brought them over to France in April 1917). Hesselink's victory was Sopwith Pup A.7340 whose pilot was Lt. S.S. Hume of No. 66 Squadron, RFC (No. 66 Squadron would not receive new equipment until October 1917 when Sopwith Camels replaced its Pups). Hume was also taken prisoner. Hesselink survived the war but Altmaier was killed in action on June 12, 1917. For both men their victories on May 27 were their first and only victories.

ghter pilot offered. That desire, his fine record to which his string of three Saxon bravery awards testified and perhaps the Paderborn experience did ... On April 20, 1917, after a brief familiarization course at the Valenciennes Fighter school, Krauss was ordered to *Jasta 27.*

When Krauss arrived at *Jasta 27,* it was under the command of *Leutnant* Philipp Wieland who had taken over after the death in action of the unit's first *Staffelführer, Leutnant* Hans von Keudell who had only been in the job a few days (see Page 201).[20.] Krauss did not get a confirmed victory until July 7. This, his first, is identified as a Spad in the unit's War Diary and as an R.E.8 in the *Nachrichtenblatt.* At least both sources agreed on the location, northwest of Ypres in Flanders, that graveyard of so many British and German aircraft. For Krauss, July would be both a good month and a frustrating one. His July 7 success was quickly followed by a second victory on the 16th when he downed a Sopwith, near Ypres again. On

July 24 he and the man who had replaced Wieland as *Jasta 27's* leader, the then-*Oberleutnant* Hermann Göring, and later *Reichsmarshall* of Hitler's 3rd Reich and head of the *Luftwaffe,* tangled with a Martinsyde. Both men put in claims. The decision was in Göring's favor, not surprising when a mere *Vizefeldwebel* was up against his Commanding Officer in the matter. It became Göring's 10th confirmed victory.[21.] July 28 was another day of disappointment for Krauss. Again he attacked a Martinsyde and again he thought he had gotten it. But it was not confirmed either.[22.] Some compensation for his efforts came on July 31 when Prussia saw fit to bestow the Iron Cross 1st Class on him.

An observation balloon destroyed on August 14 behind the ruined town of Ypres constituted Krauss' third confirmed victory. And while his official total score is everywhere carried as four, there is some confusion as to its date. Squadron records mark it down as a Spad shot down on September 20, 1917. The *Nachrichtenblatt,* although agreeing

---

[20.] After extensive service in two-seater formations including *Feldflieger-Abteilung 6* where, as a Fokker *Eindecker* pilot, he was credited with a victory on September 6, 1916, Philipp Wieland joined *Jasta 8* just six days later as one of its first members. He was appointed the Commanding Officer of *Jasta 27* on February 20,1917. With no victories in either unit he was returned to *Jasta 8* on May 20. On June 13, 1917 Wieland was wounded in the thigh. Thereafter, he had brief stints with two other *Jasta* but without result and his last known assignments were with *Armee-Flug-Park 3* and *Kofl 3* beginning on March 27, 1918.

[21.] Hermann Göring is, of course, one of the more interesting figures in the history of the 20th Century. It is not the purpose of this book to go beyond the end of World War I in describing the careers of such men. But since most of what has been written about him gives scant details of his service in World War I, the following brief re-cap may be of some interest to readers not familiar with it. His flying service in that war was long and distinguished. It started with *Artillerie-Flieger-Abteilung 203* which he joined on October 1, 1915. There he was credited with his first victory on November 16, 1915. Two more victories were scored on March 14 and July 30, 1916, a most creditable performance. Four other postings followed before the year was out - to *Feldflieger-Abteilung 25* on August 5, to *Kampfstaffel Metz* on September 9, to *Jasta 6* on September 28 and to *Jasta 5* on October 20. In an air combat on November 2, 1916 Göring was seriously wounded.

After he had recovered and an interim assignment at the end of the year at *Flieger-Ersatz-Abteilung 10* at Böblingen, he got back into action with *Jasta 26* on February 15, 1917. With this unit he added four more victories to his score, three in April and one in May 1917. Then with Phillip Wieland being eased out of the leadership of *Jasta 27,* Göring was appointed its new commander with an effective date of May 17. For the next fourteen months he led by example, scoring

all but one of his remaining victories and receiving all his major honors. He got one victory in June, two in July (including the disputed claim with Krauss) and two in August. On August 19 he was promoted *Oberleutnant.* Two more victories were recorded in September and then on October 20, with his total score standing at 15, he was awarded the Knight's Cross with Swords of the Royal Hohenzollern House Order. The next day he got his 16th victory. Only one more was added before the end of the year, this on November 7. And with only two additional victories in 1918, one in February and one in April, he received the coveted *Orden Pour le Mérite* on June 2, 1918. His score was only 18 so this was a major and undoubtedly controversial departure from the criterion then in effect by which a fighter pilot had to have at least 20 victories before his name would be considered for the award. Göring got three more victories before the month was out and then was named *Kommandeur* of *Jagdgeschwader Freiherr von Richthofen Nr. 1* on July 11. Promoted *Hauptmann,* he scored only one more victory in the war (despite his conviction that he was more valuable as a leader on the ground, he was criticized for "flying from a desk"). Göring's pre-air service unit was *4. Badisches Infanterie-Regiment Prinz Wilhelm Nr. 112* and as a consequence of that affiliation and as his record in the air merited recognition, he was awarded first the Knight's Cross, 2nd Class with Swords of the Baden Order of the Zähringer Lion and then its ultimate bravery award for officers, the exclusive Military Karl-Friedrich Merit Order in the grade of Knight.

[22.] The only Martinsyde confirmed in the *Nachrichtenblatt* on July 28, 1917 was credited to the *Flieger-Abteilung 45b* crew of *Leutnant* Hörauf and *Offizier-Stellvertreter* Sättler. They downed Martinsyde G102 A.3986 whose pilot, Capt. H.O.D. Wilkens, was taken prisoner. This action, coupled with a good overall record, resulted in Otto Sättler receiving the Bavarian Silver Bravery Medal, one of only 17 awarded to fliers for World War I.

20, 1917. The *Nachrichtenblatt,* although agreeing it was a Spad, does not show it until its list of enemy aircraft downed on January 13, 1918. Whatever the correct date, this was the end of Krauss' scoring and his chance for even higher honors from his home state. On January 19, in a combat with a British two-seater, he was himself shot down and killed.

VIZEFELDWEBEL MAX WACKWITZ

Max Wackwitz, like Krauss, was a transfer from the ground troops, joining the *Fliegertruppe* on July 11, 1915. His initial pilot training commenced at the flying school at Leipzig-Lindenthal. From April until November 1916 he served with *Feld-flieger-Abteilung 65* in the Vosges. December 1, 1916 was a signal day for him. On that day his earlier work was rewarded with the Silver Friedrich August Medal and that was also the day that he had been ordered to report to a fighter unit, in his case *Jasta 24*. The unit had been formed on October 25, 1916 but did not receive its full complement of aircraft until early January 1917.

Wackwitz's name first appears in the *Jasta 24* War Diary when it records that he was responsible for forcing an enemy plane to break off combat and dive steeply for its own lines on February 25. In another combat on April 14 his right rudder cable was cut and in this dangerous condition he gingerly made his way back to his own field at low level. His first victory was scored on May 10 when a Spad fell to him near Fichtelberg in Flanders. More than three months went by before he was again engaged in an event that warranted an entry in the War Diary. On August 26 he had an apparently successful combat with another Spad, this time over Zillebeke Lake. As he was watching is opponent fall, he came under attack himself. He was able to shake off the enemy plane but in the process, lost track of the fate of the first one. Back at his aerodrome, no independent verification of Wackwitz's victim could be found so no official credit was allowed. His luck in September improved a bit. On the 11th he bagged a Sopwith along the Ypres-Roulens road and on the 26th he shot one of the dangerous Sopwith Triplanes of the Royal Naval Air Service out of the air for his third confirmed victory.

The four-victory mark was always one of some significance to German fighter pilots. At that point they could expect to see their names begin to appear in official dispatches and on the lists of victorious pilots that were put out from time to time. So it must have been a source of some frustration when on October 7 over Houthulst Forest Wackwitz shot up both an R.E. 8 and a Sopwith Camel, apparently crippling them badly. He was unable to follow either down so again he did not observe whether they actually fell or not. And again the results had to be recorded as inconclusive. Unlike the British scoring system, there was no victory for planes "shot down out of control". It was not until December 5 that the important four victory level was reached. Wackwitz came across another R.E.8 while out on a solo patrol. This time there would be no doubt about its fate. The plane and its unfortunate crew went down in flames near Athies, for all the front to see.

Just two days later, December 7, 1917, Wackwitz was again out hunting, this time paired with a wingmate, *Unteroffizier* Kurt Reinhold, a three-victory pilot himself. They picked up a flight of three Martinsydes and Reinhold got one of them for his fourth victory.[23] His victim came down near Mercatel on the Bapaume-Arras road (on November 24 *Jasta 24* was one of the German aviation formations that had been moved down from Flanders to the Cambrai area to meet the British threat caused by their surprise and, as it turned out, short-lived success with a tank-supported infantry breakthrough). But Reinhold returned from the mission alone. Wackwitz was missing. Only later was it learned that he was safe, though a prisoner of the British. His Albatros D.V 4545/17 had been hit, apparently by ground fire, and although not seriously damaged, it was enough to force Wackwitz to put it down in enemy held territory. *Jasta 24* was further cheered by the news that came through on December 30. Wackwitz had been awarded the Silver St. Henry Medal with a citation that specifically mentioned his third victory the previous September 26. One wonders whether this news got through to him as he sat out the war in deary surroundings or whether he only found out about it upon his return to Germany after the Armistice.

---

[23] On December 10, 1917, Reinhold was on a test flight over his airfield when his aircraft suffered wing failure at a height of about 300 feet. The plane crashed, carrying Reinhold to his death.

VIZEFLUGMEISTER ERNST SCHWARZ

Land-locked Saxony produced at least one naval non-commissioned officer who earned the Silver St. Henry Medal for heroism in the air. He was *Vizeflugmeister* Ernst Schwarz who was a bit older than most of the fliers, having been born on October 22, 1887 in the small town of Eutritzsch near Leipzig. Schwarz was embarked on a merchant seaman's career and was rated a *Steuermann* (Helmsman) before the war but was in the naval reserves. He was thus called to the colors at the outbreak of hostilities but like much of the German High Seas Fleet until the Battle of Jutland (May 31/June 1, 1916), he saw no action. This changed when he wrangled a transfer to aviation and on January 19, 1916 he joined *II. Seefliegerabteilung* for pilot training.

After World War II and not long before his death, Schwarz wrote an extensive account of his wartime experiences, principally covering the period from April 5, 1917 to March 15, 1918 when he was assigned to *Seeflugstation Flandern I* at Zeebrügge. Perhaps it was the distance of time which color many reminiscences like this but he recorded many flights in these memoirs that do not match other data on German naval operations (for example, days on which he mentions patrols when, because of bad weather, there were no flight operations at all). There are also discrepancies in some of his accounts of actions in which he claimed to have participated (for example, the interceptions of neutral shipping carrying contraband which were actually carried out by others). So what he wrote has to be approached with considerable caution and for that reason, should not be relied upon to relate his story in any detail. Nonetheless, there is no doubt that he was there, took all the risks associated with flying over open water against a determined enemy and had more than his share of success. His many awards testify to that.

The honor of which *Herr* Schwarz was most proud was the Imperial German Navy *Ehrenpreis* (Prize of Honor) that he received for an aerial victory on October 1, 1917.[24] We will first mention Schwarz's statements about the incident that earned it and then add what corroborative facts there are to support them. Schwarz claimed that his *Ehrenpreis* was given in recognition of a victory over the first British Curtiss flying boat to be shot down in the war. He was in the rear seat of the float plane acting as the observer/gunner and his pilot was the then *Oberleutnant zur See* Friedrich Christiansen. Two months later, Christiansen became the first naval airman of the war to receive the *Orden Pour le Mérite* when it was bestowed on him on December 11, 1917.[25] In this case Schwarz does not seem to be embellishing the truth. The destruction of a Curtiss flying boat on October 1, 1917 is confirmed on a list of enemy aircraft shot down by German naval fliers in the Flanders area up to April 21, 1918 (as well as enemy shipping sunk or successfully intercepted by them off the coast). The men in these incidents are not named however. There is also a tabulation of victorious German naval airmen up to April 1, 1918. No victory dates are given but a *Vizeflugmeister* Schwarz, acting as an observer, is credited there with one victory. Finally, there is his *Ehrenpreis* itself. As was customary, it carries a silver plaque on which Schwarz's name, rank and the date of the victory are engraved.

Schwarz received the Silver St. Henry Medal on January 26, 1918. Earlier, he had been awarded the Friedrich August Medal in Silver, both Iron Crosses and the Hamburg Hanseatic Cross. In August 1918 he was decorated simultaneously with both the 1st Class and 2nd Class Friedrich August Cross of Oldenburg.

However his memory may have played tricks with him in his later years, it can be fairly said that Ernst Schwarz served long and well as one of the "Hornets of Zeebrügge".

---

[24] The *Ehrenpreis* was the German naval counterpart to the army *Ehrenbecher* (Goblet of Honor). Like the *Ehrenbecher,* the *Ehrenpreis* was awarded to airmen for their first victory and, as with the army award, was given to both airmen in two-seater aircraft. In the navy, it was also awarded for the destruction of enemy warships and U-boats. As the illustration shows, it was actually a small table trophy, measuring just 10" high by 4½" square. It is one of the rarest items of Imperial German aviation militaria.

[25] *Kapitänleutnant* Friedrich Christiansen ended the war with 21 victories. This score included a British coastal airship that his flight brought down in flames and a British submarine believed sunk although, in fact, it made it back to port heavily damaged and with fatalities. There were only two other naval *Pour le Mérite* airmen, *Leutnant* Theo Osterkamp with 32 victories and *Oberleutnant zur See* Gotthard Sachsenberg with 31 victories.

One of only two known naval airmen to receive the Silver St. Henry Medal, *Vizeflugmeister* Ernst Schwarz was credited with at least one victory when flying with the commander of *Seeflugstation Flandern I,* the *Pour le Mérite* and eventual 21-victory ace, *Kapitänleutnant* Friedrich Christiansen. For this, as with all successful naval fliers, Schwarz received the *Ehrenpreis* shown above with a silver plaque engraved with his name, rank and the date of the action, October 1, 1917. Despite its apparently rather heroic proportions, the trophy itself was quite small, measuring barely 10" in height. Because the German Naval Air Service was smaller than the Army Air Service and the chance for aerial victories more limited, the *Ehrenpreis* was awarded much more sparingly than the Army's *Ehrenbecher* although no official figures for total bestowals of either have ever been found.

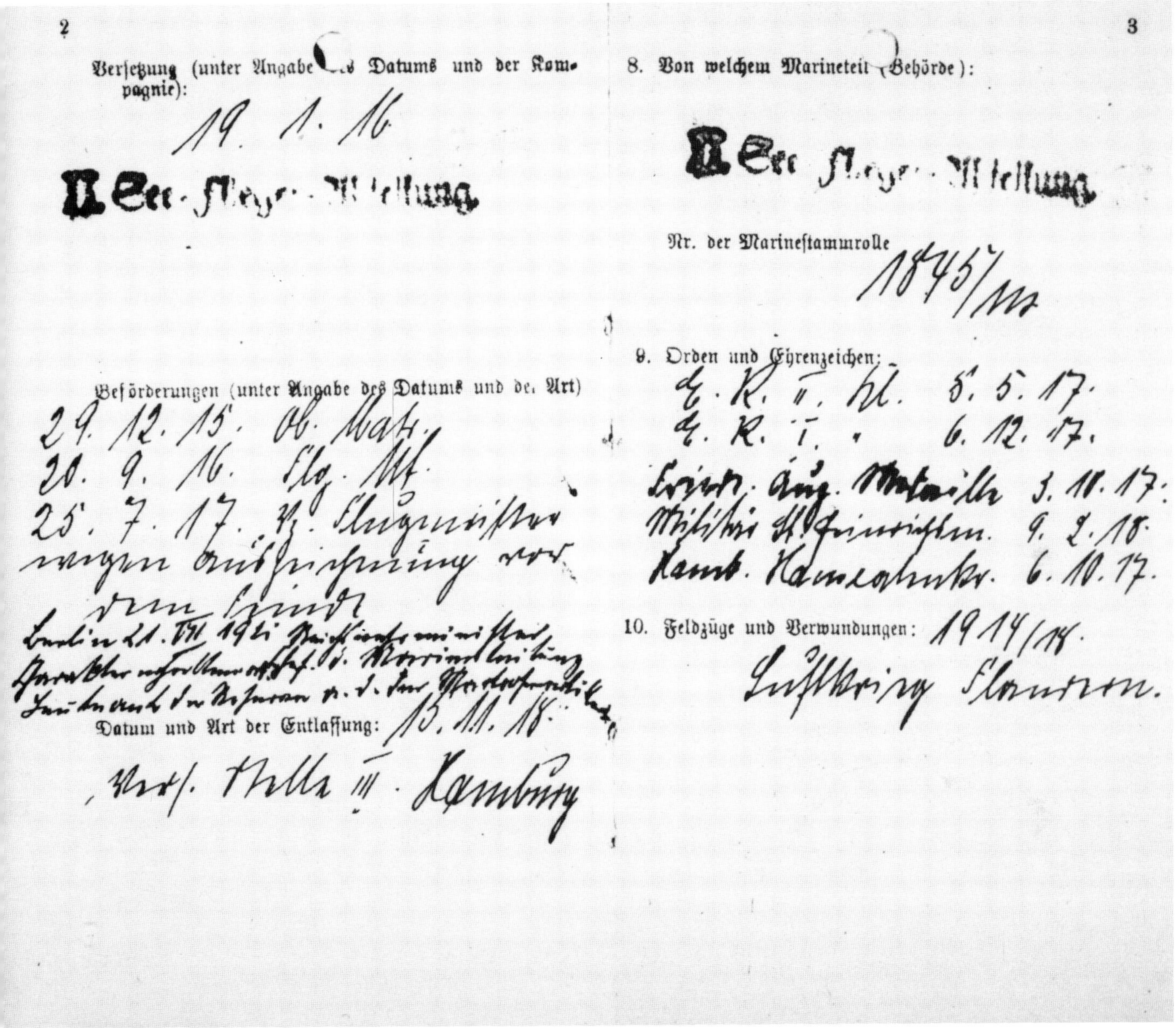

2

Verſetzung (unter Angabe ... Datums und der Kom-
pagnie):

19. 1. 16

II See-Flieger-Abteilung

Beförderungen (unter Angabe des Datums und der Art)

29. 12. 15. Ob. Mat.
20. 9. 16. Flg. Mt.
25. 7. 17. Fl. Flugmeister
wegen Auszeichnung vor
dem Feind

Berlin 21. VII. 1917 ...
...
...

Datum und Art der Entlaſſung: *15. 11. 18.*

Ers. Abt. II Hamburg

8. Von welchem Marineteil (Behörde):

II See-Flieger-Abteilung

Nr. der Marineſtammrolle

1845/M

9. Orden und Ehrenzeichen:

E. K. u. Kl. 5. 5. 17.
E. K. I. . 6. 12. 17.
Friedr. Aug. Medaille 3. 11. 17.
Militär St. Heinrichm. 9. 2. 18.
Hamb. Hanseatenkr. 6. 10. 17.

10. Feldzüge und Verwundungen: *1914/18.*

Luftkrieg Flandern.

This exerpt from *Vizeflugmeister* Ernst Schwarz's service records shows, on the left, his various promotions and, on the right, the awards he earned. This indicates that he received the Iron Cross, 2nd Class on May 5, 1917, the Iron Cross, 1st Class on December 6, 1917, the Friedrich August Medal (undoubtedly in Silver) on October 3, 1917, the Military St. Henry Medal (in Silver) on February 9, 1918 (another record dates the award from January 26, 1918; such slight discrepencies are not uncommon between various records) and the Hamburg Hanseatic Cross on October 6, 1917. Not as yet entered here are the Oldenburg Friedrich August Cross in both 1st and 2nd Class which Schwarz received in August 1918. Schwarz may have embellished his career (see text) but there is no doubt he was a highly decorated airman.

Offizier-Stellvertreter Karl Becksmann put his pre-war flying and aircraft design experience to good work when war came. In the process he amassed a truly remarkable number of frontline combat missions and flights as a test pilot later. Along the way he earned the Silver St. Henry Medal as well as the Friedrich August Medal in Silver from Saxony. Becksmann joined *Feldflieger-Abteilung 22* on May 13, 1915, transferred to *Flieger-Abteilung (A)252* in 1917 and after 420 reconnaissance and artillery cooperation sorties was sent to *Armee-Flugpark 1* on September 24, 1917. He remained there until the end of the war and for his brilliant record he was awarded the Prussian Golden Military Merit Cross on February 14, 1918 upon the occasion of his 1,000th flight at *AFP 1*. In the photograph at left he is seen at *FFl.Abt. 22* with a Rumpler C.I and at right with a D.F.W. C.V at *AFP I* at Rethel.

nan Army Air Service's fighter pilots in the spring of 1917, he would have been an almost sure candidate for the award of a Gold St. Henry Medal.

VIZEFELDWEBEL KARL SCHLEGEL

Karl Schlegel was intending to become a career non-commissioned officer in the Royal Saxon Army and already early in the war he had demonstrated that he would make a very good one. As an *Unteroffizier* in *Maschinengewehr-Abteilung 8* his bravery had earned him the Silver St. Henry Medal early in 1915 (his award was on a list dated April 25, 1915 in *Sachsen in grosser Zeit*). In the spring of 1917 he volunteered for the *Fliegertruppe,* was accepted and then began a rather long period of training and service behind the front before he made it to a combat assignment. But when he did, he proved himself to be a redoubtable fighter pilot, one of a select few who made the destruction of enemy observation balloons their specialty.

Flieger-Ersatz-Abteilung 1 at Altenburg was the scene of Schlegel's initial flight training and this was followed by more experience at *FEA 4* at Halle. At his next stop, *FEA 6* at Grossenhain, he was engaged in test flying of aircraft. Finally, at the beginning of May 1918 he was sent to *Kampfeinsitzer-Staffel 1* for a few days of fighter familiarization. From there he joined *Jasta 45* whose leader, *Leutnant* Hans Joachim Rolfes, had the distinction of leading the unit from its inception on December 23, 1917 until the end of the war.[29] Schlegel was to pair up there with another

non-commissioned officer pilot, *Offizier-Stellvertreter* Gustav Doerr, and with whom he established a friendly rivalry for top scoring honors reminiscent of that which characterized the Immelmann/Boelcke relationship back in the *Feldflieger-Abteilung 62* days of 1915 and 1916. As with that earlier competition, one was always slightly ahead of the other, in this case Doerr, as he and Schlegel began to amass victories at a rapid rate in July, August and September 1918.[30]

Schlegel's first victory came on June 14 when he destroyed an observation balloon, the first of a total of 14 of them with which he was ultimately credited. He burned five more balloons in July and shot down six aircraft, four Bréguets and two Spads. Many fighter pilots thought balloons, protected as they were with heavy ground defenses and often by roving patrols of fighters, and a well-flown two-seater like a Bréguet were far more dangerous targets than a single enemy fighter plane. August was almost as productive for Schlegel as July was. Again the score was five more balloons and, this time, two Spads. The early days of September saw the furious action in the air continue. By the 5th he had gotten two more of the big gas bags and another Spad. This brought his score to 22 at a time when his comrade, Doerr, had just gotten his 25th. Interestingly, in view of Schlegel's victory mix, Doerr had not a single balloon to his credit. All of his victories had been aircraft, mostly Bréguets and Spads. Then, while Doerr continued to widen the gap between their respective scores, Schlegel experienced a dry spell for a couple of weeks and then went on leave on September 25.

---

[29] Hans Joachim Rolfes had flown in three flights of *Kampfgeschwader 2* from October 5, 1916 through February 19, 1917, *Kampfstaffeln 10, 11* and *12*. There he earned his Pilot's Badge on January 30, 1917. Just before he left *Kasta 11,* on February 17, he was involved in a combat with a Voisin two-seater which was forced down on the other side of the lines and consequently, not confirmed. He was posted to *Jasta 32* on February 20 and got his first victory on July 6 when he shot down a Farman. This brought the award of the Iron Cross, 1st Class on July 23. His actual date of appointment to lead *Jasta 45* was December 17, 1917 and throughout his tenure he was a steady and consistent scorer and was credited with an eventual total of 17 confirmed victories. He was awarded the Knight's Cross with Swords of the Royal Hohenzollern House Order on an unknown date.

[30] Gustav Doerr's total victory score officially was 35, all achieved in *Jasta 45* which he joined in Feburary 1918 after service in *Feldflieger-Abteilung 68* (beginning in March 1916) and *Feldflieger-Abteilung 6 / Flieger-Abteilung (A)257* (beginning in July 1916). Doerr had only two confirmed victories when Schlegel arrived at *Jasta 45* but the tempo quickly

picked up. Another victory was added in late May and his production was doubled in June when three more planes, all Spads, were brought down by him. July saw 11 victories, his best single month. After reaching the 23-victory level on August 24, he was awarded the highest Prussian bravery award for non-commissioned officers on August 29, the Golden Military Merit Cross. Seven more victories were recorded in September, five in October and one in November (although one of these did not receive official confirmation). As he continued to perform brilliantly after the award of the Golden Military Merit Cross, his effectiveness was rewarded with promotion to *Leutnant* and on October 25 Doerr was nominated for the *Orden Pour le Mérite*. The war ended before any action on the proposal could be taken and he never received the award as a result. Doerr had two serious mishaps during his flying career. On June 10, 1917 in *Flieger-Abteilung (A)257* he was shot down, his observer was killed and he suffered a badly broken lower jaw. On May 28, 1918 in the combat where he scored his third victory, he brought his plane down burning for a landing between the lines.

Unser erfolgreicher Kampfflieger
Leutnant Frickart

Reflections from the studio lights in this formal portrait photo-
graph of *Leutnant* Wilhelm Frickart make positive identification impossible but it seems almost certain that the second and
third medals on his bar after the Iron Cross, 2nd Class are the
Silver St. Henry Medal and the Friedrich August Medal respec-
tively. The last two medals are Austrian Bravery Medals, the
Silver Medal, 2nd Class and the Bronze Medal, both in the
Emperor Karl pattern which coinage came in April 1917.
Frickart earned these Austrian awards with *Flieger-Abteilung
(A)242* on the Eastern Front and before he was commissioned
on October 24, 1917. There he scored his first five victories, two
Voisins in April 1917 and three balloons in June of that year.

Frickart then served in *Fl.Abt. (A)220* before joining *Jasta 38*
in February 1918. With *Jasta 38* he scored a sixth victory in
March and in that month and in April he forced two Sopwiths
to land in enemy lines. Transferred to *Jasta 64* in July on the
Western Front, he spent only one month with it before going to
Jasta 65. His next confirmed victory was on August 30 and his
last three, bringing his total to 10 confirmed, were scored in
September. Frickart also claimed four balloons in the Brzezany
area on the Eastern Front, all on June 28, 1917, but these, like
the two planes forced down, were never officially confirmed.

here is the possibility of another aviation recipient of the Honor Cross with Swords. He was a *Vizefeldwebel* Hillner, a pilot in *Bogohl 3*, the Gotha bomber squadron whose main mission was air attacks on England. The caption next to his photograph that appears here explains that speculation also.

The Friedrich August Medals

On April 23, 1905, soon after he ascended the throne, King Friedrich August III established the Friedrich August Medal in two grades, Silver and Bronze. They were meant to recognize meritorious accomplishments both in peacetime and in war by military personnel from the rank of *Feldwebel* and below and by civilians of comparable station acting in official capacities.[1] The medals in both grades were identical with only the finish differentiating between them. In terms of precedence, they ranked below all the other Saxon military decorations discussed so far.

The obverse of the medals carried the entwined initials *FAR* standing for *FRIEDRICH AUGUST REX*, above which there was a royal crown. These elements were encircled by a laurel wreath. On the reverse, on two lines, the lettering *FRIEDRICH AUGUST / MEDAILLE* appeared. Above and below this was scalloped scroll work incorporating three upturned leaves and four pearl drops on each. Different ribbons were employed depending upon the nature of the award. For wartime awards the ribbon was yellow gold with two light blue side stripes, these being the military colors of Saxony (as opposed to the national colors of green and white), as reflected in the ribbons of the Military St. Henry Order and the campaign commemorative decorations of 1849, 1863/64 and 1866. In peacetime the ribbon was also yellow gold but with two black side stripes and a thinner black center stripe. From May 22, 1916, awards to civilians for war-related service in the homeland carried a metal device affixed to the peacetime ribbon with the raised lettering *WELTKRIEG 1914-16*. For men the device was a rectangular bar. For women it was an ornamental oak leaf.

Ranking as it did at the low end of the scale of Saxon bravery awards for the troops, it was by far the most frequently awarded. The sheer volume of likely awards plus the exigencies of time and higher priorities meant that no effort was made to establish these numbers in the records of the *Staatsarchiv* in Dresden. Consequently, no comprehensive list of aviation recipients is possible at this time. But in the earlier issues of the German flying magazine, *Flugsport*, a goodly number of such awards appear. In 1915, when they first began to show up, seven awards of the Silver and 15 of the Bronze to men in the air service were reported. In 1916 there were mentions of 13 Silver awards and nine Bronze. Then, as the numbers of all awards given out as the war progressed made it impractical to list anything except the more important honors, *Flugsport* reported only three awards of the Silver in 1917 and none at all in 1918.[2] Even in 1915 and 1916, the total of 44 awards that made it into print was probably only a fraction of those going to fliers and ground crew personnel. The usual pattern was that from the rank of *Unteroffizier* and up, the Silver was awarded. Men with the two lowest ranks, *Flieger* and *Gefreiter*, would receive the Bronze. Since the enlisted men on actual flying status tended to hold the higher non-commissioned officer ranks, we can assume that many of the Bronze awards went to ground crew personnel.

Despite its commonness, the Silver Friedrich August Medal could still be a hard-earned award. That would be particularly true for a man not of Saxon birth. No better example of this exists than the one given to *Offizier-Stellvertreter* Friedrich Altemeier. He received his as a direct result of his unit, *Jasta 24*, being designated a Saxon

---

[1] The Friedrich August Medal was also given to men with the rank of *Fähnrich* (Ensign), as in the case of Max Immelmann just before he was commissioned.

[2] In the early stages of the war, *Flugsport* even listed awards of the Iron Cross, 2nd Class. This had to be

abandoned as the numbers became unmanageable. By 1918, the only award that generally made its pages was the *Orden Pour le Mérite*. The *Militär-Wochenblatt* is of little help either. It almost completely ignored mentioning Saxon awards throughout its wartime issues.

These two photographs, taken in quick succession indicate that *Leutnant* Werner Voss was, in fact, in the cockpit of this Fokker Triplane and that his head and shoulders were not stripped in later. Note in the photograph above his *Pour le Mérite* is not evident. In the photograph below he has turned just enough to give us a glimpse of the badge at his throat. This also strongly suggests that the headrest, too, was present and not later touched in.

That could have been the reason the award never came, as was the case with three other nominees whose capture ended their chances to receive the award. These men were *Leutnant* Paul Billik, *Oberleutnant* Maximilian von Cossel and *Hauptmann* Eduard Wolfgang Zorer.

Page 151: According to a *Kofl 6* report, *Vizefeldwebel* Sebastian Festner was killed in action on April 25, 1917.

Page 178: At the time Volume II was published, no photograph of *Vizefeldwebel* August Begemann was available. Now, thanks to the same source who provided the two photographs of Fritz Kuhlmann, two fine ones on Begemann appear here.

Page 190: "*Offz.-Stv.* Paul Leim, *Feldflieger-Abteilung 300*" should read "*Offz.-Stv.* Paul Leim, *Flieger-Abteilung 300.*"

Page 192: In the photograph at the upper left, the pilot with the *Pour le Mérite* observer, *Leutnant* Albert Müller-Kahle, can now be positively identified as *Vizefeldwebel* Ernst Nitschmann. Müller-Kahle also received the Knight 2nd Class with Swords of the Albert Order and as a consequence of there being little photographic material on him and the question raised when the photograph appeared in Volume II as to the identity of the pilot, it has been used again in this volume (see Page 176).

Page 231: Even though the award was not present on the *Ordenskissen* of *Hauptmann* Oswald Boelcke at his funeral ceremonies in Cambrai, research at the *Staatsarchiv* Weimar, *Aussenstelle* Gotha has established the fact that he did, in fact, receive the Knight's Cross, 1st Class with Swords of the Ernestine House Order from Saxe-Coburg and Gotha on July 31, 1916.

Page 238: To the awards of *Leutnant* Lothar *Freiherr* von Richthofen the War Medal of the Ottoman Empire should be added.

Page 242: To the awards of *Hauptmann* Ernst Brandenburg the Knight's Cross, 1st Class with Swords of the Ernestine House Order from Saxe-Coburg and Gotha should be added. He received it on July 30, 1918.

Page 243: To the awards of *Hauptmann* Rudolf Kleine the Knight's Cross, 2nd Class with Swords of the Ernestine House Order from Saxe-Coburg and Gotha should replace the Reuss Honor Cross, 3rd Class with Crown and Swords. The Reuss piece was misidentified when examining the photograph of his *Ordenskissen* which appears in the photograph on Page 208 of Volume II. Kleine received his Ernestine House Order on December 14, 1914 as an *Oberleutnant* in *Feldflieger-Abteilung 9.*

Page 244: The known awards of *Leutnant* Wilhelm Schreiber were inadvertently omitted. They were:

> *Orden Pour le Mérite* - Prussia
> Royal Hohenzollern House Order, Knight's Cross with Swords - Prussia
> Iron Cross, 1st and 2nd Class - Prussia
> Friedrich August Cross, 1st and 2nd Class - Oldenburg
> Hanseatic Cross - Hamburg
> Observer's Badge - Germany

Page 257: From the information provided earlier regarding a correction on Page 38 of Volume I, it is evident that the date of February 5, 1918 for the award of the Knight's Cross with Swords of the Royal Hohenzollern House Order to *Leutnant* Hans *Ritter* von Adam is not correct. Although the precise date has not yet been established, it was before he was killed in action on November 15, 1917, not after it.

Page 257: In his own book, *Oberleutnant* Walter Aschoff states that his Hohenzollern House Order was awarded on December 4, 1917, not on December 14, 1917. However, such minor discrepancies in dates, give or take a

Vizefeldwebel August Begemann, standing on the right, of *Flieger-Abteilung 6* was awarded the Golden Military Merit Cross on April 11, 1918. The observer here on Begemann's right may be *Leutnant* Doetsch with whom he was known to have flown in 1918. The pin-back badge Begemann is wearing to the side of his Iron Cross, 1st Class and his Pilot's Badge is the War Honor Cross for Heroic Deeds from the Principality of Lippe.

Begemann perching on the fuselage of a D.F.W. C.V. during the winter of 1917/1918. The man on the ground is the same observer with whom Begemann posed in the photograph above.

few days, are frequently encountered.

Page 257: *"Oblt. z. See* Wilhelm Baumbach" should read *"Oblt.* Wilhelm Baumbach."

Page 258: Walter Boenicke's rank was *Leutnant.*

Page 258: *"Hptm.* Oskar *Freiherr* von Boenigk" should read *"Oblt.* Oskar *Freiherr* von Boenigk.

Page 258: *Hauptmann* Cranz's first name was Friedrich.

Page 259: *Leutnant* Drum's first name was Karl.

Page 259: *Oberleutnant* Fischer's first name was Veit.

Page 259: *"Oblt.* Eberhard Gandert" should read *"Oblt.* Hans-Eberhard Gandert."

Page 260: The date of the Hohenzollern House Order awarded to *Leutnant* Hempel was November 9, 1918.

Page 261: The rank and first name of the Jeschonnek listed was *Leutnant* Hans.

Page 262: Apparently, *Jasta 6* should be added to the units in which *Hauptmann* Bruno Loerzer served. One record states that he joined *Jasta 6* on September 6, 1916

and was posted out on February 4, 1917 to take the command of *Jasta 26.* However, other records state that in between those dates he had brief stints with both *Jasta 5* and *Jasta 17.*

Page 264: *"Hptm.* Günther Schwartzkof" should read *"Lt.* Günther Schwartzkof."

Page 264: The name of *Hauptmann* Karl Schweikhardt can also be found spelled as Carl Schweikhardt and Carl Schweikhard.

Page 265: The first name of *Hauptmann* Súren was Walter.

Front Cover:
It was stated that the items shown on all four color covers of Volume II were the property of the Foundation for Aviation World War I. Subsequently, a printing error required a new photograph of the *Pour le Mérite* shown on the front cover. So that production would not be unduly delayed, a badge had to be borrowed from a collector since the Foundation's badge that was originally used was not available. The collector's generosity in allowing this switch to be made is hereby gratefully acknowledged.

Note: Corrections and comments concerning this Volume III will also be greatly appreciated.

.t. Hans Donath	*Fl.Abt. (A)213*	January 7, 1918
.t. Lothar Nagel	*I. Mar. Küsten Fl.Abt.*	January 26, 1918
)blt. Hermann Martini	*Jasta 12*	Febraury 6, 1918
.t. Erich von Neindorff	*Fl.Abt. (A)284*	February 9, 1918
)blt. Edmund von Glass	*Fl.Abt. (A)232*	March 18, 1918
.t. Friedrich Freytag	*Fl.Abt. 9*	March 23, 1918
)blt. Egon Doerstling	*Bogohl 7*	May 1, 1918
.t. Hermann Kottwitz	*Fl.Abt. (A)239*	May 31, 1918
.t. Kurt Scheibe	*Bogohl 1*	May 31, 1918
)blt. Georg Henke	*Schlasta 18*	June 10, 1918
.t. Otto Creutzmann	*Jasta 43*	July 19, 1918
.t. Werner Heine	*Fl.Abt. (A)276*	July 19, 1918
.t. Gerhard Heym	*Fl.Abt. (A)233*	July 19, 1918
)blt. Karl Persch	*Bosta 7, Bogohl 6*	September 1, 1918
.t. Max Stopf	*Fl.Abt. (A)272*	September 1, 1918
.t. Franz Büchner	*Jasta 13*	October 7, 1918
Rittm. Walter Heymann	*Fl.Abt. (A)256*	October 7, 1918
.t. Walter Noack	*Jasta 29*	October 7, 1918
.t. Hermann Schaue	*Fl.Abt. (A)222*	October 17, 1918
.t. Guenther von Büren	*Jasta 18*	October 24, 1918
.t. Karl Höhne	*Fl.Abt. (A)248*	October 29, 1918
.t. Karl Töpfer	*Fl.Abt. (A)253*	July 1920
.t. Walter Dietrich	*Fl.Abt. (A)222*	October 1922

Source: *"Der Königlich Sächsische Militär-St. Heinrichs-Orden 1736-1918"*

[1.] See the citation to Walter von Bülow on Page 122 and subsequent commentary on the conflicting details therein.

Appendix III

Officers of the Imperial German Air Force Who Received the Knight's
Cross of the Saxon Military St. Henry Order for Aerial Action, 1914-1922

(Arranged Alphabetically)

Rank at Time of Award and Name of Recipient	Unit in Which Recipient Served At Time of Award	Date of Award
Oblt. Hans Baldamus	*Art.Fl.Abt. 201*	September 26, 1916
Lt. Wilhelm Baumbach	*II. Mar.FFl.Abt.*	May 11, 1917
Oblt. Rudolf Berthold	*FFl.Abt. 23*	April 8, 1916
Rittm. Werner *Freiherr* von Beschwitz	*FFl.Abt. 39*	August 3, 1916
Lt. Karl Birch-Hirschfeld	*KS 9, KG 2*	May 26, 1916
Hptm. Eberhard Bohnstedt	*FFl.Abt. 23*	July 4, 1915
Lt. Erich Bonde	*BAO*	July 18, 1915
Lt. Hans-Joachim Buddecke	*FFl.Abt. 23*	October 16, 1915
Lt. Franz Büchner	*Jasta 13*	October 7, 1918
Lt. Walter von Bülow	*Jasta 36*	October 7, 1917[1]
Lt. Guenther von Büren	*Jasta 18*	October 24, 1918
Oblt. Karl *Freiherr* von dem Busche-Streithorst	*FFl.Abt. 63*	December 24, 1915
Lt. Hans Clausen	*Fl.Abt. (A)230*	November 4, 1917
Oblt. Emil Clemens	*FFl.Abt. 24*	November 17, 1914
Lt. Otto Creutzmann	*Jasta 43*	July 19, 1918
Lt. Walter Dietrich	*Fl.Abt. (A)222*	October 1922
Rittm. Paul Dietze	*FFl.Abt. 24*	September 4, 1915
Oblt. Egon Doerstling	*Bogohl 7*	May 1, 1918
Lt. Hans Donath	*Fl.Abt. (A)213*	January 7, 1918
Lt. Fritz Einenckel	*Fl.Abt. (A)237*	November 4, 1917
Lt. Paul Erbguth	*Jasta 30*	December 2, 1917
Oblt. Hermann Fahrig	*Fl.Abt. (A)244*	June 2, 1917
Lt. Harald Förster	*Fl.Abt. (A)210*	March 4, 1917
Lt. Philipp Franke	*Art.Fl.Abt. 201*	June 13, 1916
Lt. Friedrich Freytag	*Fl.Abt. 9*	March 23, 1918
Lt. Kurt Fritzsche	*Fl.Abt. 300*	September 21, 1917
Hptm. Gert-Wolf Froehlich	*Fl.Abt. (A)226*	July 24, 1917
Oblt. Gottfried Glaeser	*FFl.Abt. 23*	July 4, 1915
Oblt. Edmund von Glass	*Fl.Abt. (A)232*	March 18, 1918
Lt. Hans-Gottfried von Haebler	*Fl.Abt. (A)273*	October 2, 1917
Oblt. Erich Hahn	*Jasta 19*	December 27, 1916
Lt. Erich Hahn	*Fl.Abt. 21*	April 29, 1917

Lt. Karl Hansen	FFl.Abt. 62	August 25, 1915
Lt. Rudolf Hasenohr	FFl.Abt. 24	November 17, 1914
Oblt. Erwin Haucke	Art.Fl.Abt. 219	June 13, 1916
Oblt. Wilhelm Haupt	FFl.Abt. 47	June 13, 1916
Lt. Werner Heine	Fl.Abt. (A)276	July 19, 1918
Lt. Alfred Helm	KS 30, KG 5	January 10, 1917
Oblt. Georg Henke	Schlasta 18	June 10, 1918
Oblt. Max Herrmann-Millington	Fl.Abt. (A)264	December 2, 1917
Lt. Friedrich von Hesler	FFl.Abt. 31	December 23, 1914
Lt. Martin Heydrich	Schusta 11	July 24, 1917
Lt. Gerhard Heym	Fl.Abt. (A)233	July 19, 1918
Rittm. Walter Heymann	Fl.Abt. (A)256	October 7, 1918
Lt. Karl Höhne	Fl.Abt. (A)248	October 29, 1918
Lt. Reinold Hultzsch	Art.Fl.Abt. 210	May 29, 1916
Lt. Max Immelmann	FFl.Abt. 62	October 13, 1915
Hptm. Horst Jerrmann	FFl.Abt. 8	January 31, 1917
Lt. Siegfried Kässberg	FFl.Abt. 3	July 7, 1915
Oblt. Franz Kästner	FFl.Abt. 12	June 30, 1915
Lt. Herbert Kettner	KS 25, KG 5	June 22, 1916
Lt. Johannes Kinzelmann	Jasta 7	November 11, 1917
Rittm. Kurt Kloetzer	Fl.Abt. 11	April 2, 1917
Oblt. Friedrich Knab	KG 5	September 23, 1916
Oblt. Oskar Knofe	Grufl 1	March 21, 1917
Lt. Walter Köhler	Fl.Abt. 3	July 16, 1917
Lt. Robert Koerner	Fl.Abt. (A)210	March 4, 1917
Lt. Hermann Kottwitz	Fl.Abt. (A)239	May 31, 1918
Lt. Egbert Kühn	FFl.Abt. 3	November 11, 1914
Hptm. Ernst Kunz	FFl.Abt. 33	April 14, 1916
Lt. Johannes Leistner	FFl.Abt. 59	January 12, 1916
Oblt. Rudolf Lochmann	Fl.Abt. (A)214	August 1, 1917
Hptm. Albert von Malortie	FFl.Abt. 63	December 24, 1915
Oblt. Hermann Martini	Jasta 12	February 6, 1918
Lt. Kurt Menzel	FFl.Abt. 12	February 9, 1915
Oblt. Kurt Messow	Schusta 8	November 21, 1917
Oblt. Willy Meyer	FFl.Abt. 23	July 4, 1915
Lt. Martin Möbius	Fl.Abt. (A)211	June 22, 1917
Oblt. Kurt Müller	FFl.Abt. 24	November 17, 1914
Lt. Otto Müller	Fl.Abt. 24	September 3, 1917
Lt. Lothar Nagel	I. Mar.Küsten Fl.Abt.	January 26, 1918
Lt. Erich von Neindorff	Fl.Abt. (A)284	February 9, 1918
Lt. Gerhard Nette	FFl.Abt. 12	November 17, 1914
Lt. Walter Noack	Jasta 29	October 7, 1918
Oblt. Karl Persch	Bosta 7, Bogohl 6	September 1, 1918
Lt. Werner Pfeil	FFl.Abt. 59	July 3, 1916
Rittm. Prinz Friedrich Sigismund of Prussia	Fl.Abt. 22	December 3, 1917
Lt. Johannes Reichel	FEA 1 (Austrian)	September 4, 1915
Lt. Gerhard Richter	Fl.Abt. (A)266	August 26, 1917
Oblt. Manfred Freiherr von Richthofen	Jasta 11	April 16, 1917
Lt. Kurt Rödel	FFl.Abt. 58	July 18, 1915
Oblt. Kurt Roesler	FFl.Abt. 24	November 17, 1916
Lt. Werner Roloff	Fl.Abt. (A)211	June 22, 1917

Hptm. Meinhard Rosenmüller	*FFl.Abt. 24*	September 4, 1915
Lt. Hermann Schaue	*Fl.Abt. (A)222*	October 17, 1918
Lt. Kurt Scheibe	*Bogohl 1*	May 31, 1918
Lt. Paul Schirdewahn	*Fl.Abt. 28*	October 27, 1917
Lt. Julius Schmidt	*Jasta 3*	November 11, 1917
Oblt. Hans Schneider	*FFl.Abt. 69*	September 30, 1915
Lt. Kurt Schneider	*Jasta 5*	July 24, 1917
Lt. Achatz *Graf* von der Schulenburg	*FFl.Abt. 40*	December 1, 1916
Hptm. Karl Seber	*FFl.Abt. 23*	July 4, 1915
Lt. Hans-Joachim von Seydlitz-Gerstenberg	*FFl.Abt. 23*	April 8, 1916
Oblt. Ernst Sieverts	*FFl.Abt. 62*	May 29, 1916
Hptm. Paul Sommer	*KS 10, KG 2*	May 3, 1917
Lt. Kurt von Stieglitz	*Fl.Abt. (A)278*	February 16, 1917
Lt. Max Stopf	*Fl.Abt. (A)272*	September 1, 1918
Oblt. Viktor Stresemann	*FFl.Abt. 59*	January 12, 1916
Lt. Hans Thümmler	*Art.Fl.Abt. 201*	June 22, 1916
Lt. Karl Töpfer	*Fl.Abt. (A)253*	July 1920
Lt. Walter Utermann	*Fl.Abt. 71*	March 16, 1917
Lt. Friedrich Wagner	*Fl.Abt. (A)226*	August 5, 1917
Lt. Max Wilhelmi	*FFl.Abt. 29*	October 6, 1916
Oblt. Lothar Wilisch	*FFl.Abt. 24*	July 22, 1916
Lt. Georg Zeumer	*FFl.Abt. 4*	November 17, 1914
Lt. Johannes Ziegler	*Fl.Abt. (A)273*	October 2, 1917
Lt. Georg von Zobel	*FFl.Abt. 39*	September 12, 1916

Source: *"Der Königlich Sächsische Militär-St. Heinrichs-Orden 1736-1918"*

[1.] See the citation to Walter von Bülow on Page 122 and subsequent commentary on the conflicting details therein.

Appendix XIII

Non-Commissioned Officers of the Imperial German Air Force Who Received the Saxon Gold St. Henry Medal for Aerial Action

Rank at Time of Award and Name of Recipient	Unit in Which Recipient Served at Time of Award	Date of Award
Offizier-Stellvertreter Rudolf Sattler	*Flieger-Abteilung (A)278*	February 28, 1917
Offizier-Stellvertreter Paul Aue	*Jagdstaffel 10*	July 24, 1917
Vizefeldwebel Walter Dittrich	*Jagdstaffel 1*	July 24, 1917

Source; *"Ehrenbuch der Inhaber der Sächs. Goldenen Militär-St. Heinrichs-Medaille"*

Appendix XIV

Partial List of Non-Commissioned Officers of the Imperial German Air Force
Who Received the Silver St. Henry Medal, 1915-1918

(In Order of Listing)[1]

Rank at Time of Award and Name of Recipient	Unit in Which Recipient Served at Time of Award	Date of Listing[1]
Vzfw. _____ Gelhorn	*Feldflieger-Abteilung 24*	November 30, 1915
Unteroffz. _____ Hochmuth	*Feldflieger-Abteilung 24*	February 24, 1916
Vzfw. Rudolf Sattler	*Feldflieger-Abteilung 29*	March 7, 1916
Vzfw. _____ Danneberg	*Feldflieger-Abteilung 29*	July 18, 1916
Vzfw. _____ Bachmann	*Feldflieger-Abteilung 34*	September 3, 1916
Unteroffz. Karl Kretschmer	*Feldflieger-Abteilung 17*	September 6, 1916
Unteroffz. _____ Weisse	*Feldflieger-Abteilung 67*	September 26, 1916
Vzfw. Otto Schilling	*Feldflieger-Abteilung 39*	October 21, 1916
Vzfw. Rudolf Windisch	*Feldflieger-Abteilung 62*	October 21, 1916
Unteroffz. Richard (?) Herberg	*in einer Flieger-Abteilung*[2]	February 1, 1917
Vzfw. _____ Roitzsch	*in einer Flieger-Abteilung*[3]	February 14, 1917
Vzfw. Walter Dittrich	*Jagdstaffel 1*	February 14, 1917
Unteroffz. Max Krauss	*Feldflieger-Abteilung (A)225*	February 21, 1917
Vzfw. Albert Glänzel	*Kampfgeschwader 1*	April 6, 1917
Vzfw. Paul Aue	*Jagdstaffel 10*	April 6, 1917
Vzfw. Otto(?) Fleischmann	*in einer Flieger-Abteilung*[4]	April 15, 1917
Unteroffz. _____ Kausch	*in einer Flieger-Station*	April 15, 1917
Vzfw. _____ Sattler	*in einer Flieger-Abteilung*	May 20, 1917
Unteroffz. _____ Schulz	*in einer Flieger-Abteilung*[5]	May 20, 1917
Vzfw. _____ Mehlorn	*in einer Flieger-Abteilung*	June 17, 1917
Vzfw. _____ Grundmann	*in einer Flieger-Abteilung*	August 17, 1917
Vzfw. Fritz (?) Krebs	*in einer Jagdstaffel (Jasta 6?)*	September 16, 1917
Vzfw. _____ Kiessling	*in einem Kampfgeschwader*	October 21, 1917
Vzfw. _____ Schäfer	*in einer Flieger-Abteilung*	October 24, 1917
Vzfw. _____ Otto	*in einer Flieger-Abteilung*	November 18, 1917
Vzfw. _____ Kiehle	*in einer Flieger-Abteilung*	November 18, 1917
Vzfw. _____ Bergmann	*in einer Flieger-Abteilung*	November 18, 1917
Vzfw. _____ Liehr	*in einer Flieger-Abteilung*	December 4, 1917
Vzfw. _____ Fritsche	*in einer Flieger-Abteilung*	December 4, 1917
Feldw.-Lt. _____ Schubert	*in einer Flieger-Formation*	March 24, 1918
Vzfw. _____ Rossberg	*in einer Flieger-Formation*	March 24, 1918
Vzfw. _____ Engelmann	*in einer Flieger-Formation*	March 24, 1918

Vzfw. Arno Schickel	*Flieger-Abteilung 15*	March 24, 1918
Vzfw. _____ Kopla	*in einer Flieger-Formation*	March 24, 1918
Vzfw. _____ Fleischer	*in einer Flieger-Formation*	May 16, 1918
Vzfw. _____ Beyer	*in einer Flieger-Formation*	May 16, 1918
Vzfw. _____ Schmidt	*in einer Flieger-Formation*	May 16, 1918
Vzfw. _____ Rode	*in einer Flieger-Formation*	May 16, 1918
Vzfw. _____ Lorenz	*in einer Flieger-Formation*	May 16, 1918
Vzfw. _____ Hertel	*in einer Flieger-Formation*	May 16, 1918
Vzfw. _____ Muehle	*in einer Flieger-Formation*	May 16, 1918
Vzfw. _____ Rodschinka	*in einer Flieger-Formation*	May 16, 1918
Vzfw. _____ Dietrich	*in einer Flieger-Formation*	May 16, 1918
Vzwachtm. _____ Kroehnert	*in einer Flieger-Formation*	May 16, 1918
Vzfw. _____ Görling	*in einer Flieger-Formation*	May 16, 1918
Vzfw. _____ Bochmann	*in einer Flieger-Formation*	May 16, 1918
Vzfw. Max Wackwitz	*Jagdstaffel 24*	May 16, 1918
Obersteurm. _____ Sünderhauf	*in einer Flieger-Formation*	May 16, 1918
Unteroffz. _____ Bauer	*in einer Flieger-Formation*	May 16, 1918
Gefr. _____ Seidel	*in einer Flieger-Formation*	May 16, 1918
Unteroffz. _____ Steinert	*in einer Flieger-Formation*	July 21, 1918
Vzfw. _____ Flemming	*in einer Flieger-Formation*	August 18, 1918
Vzfw. _____ Schmiedel	*in einer Flieger-Formation*	October 1, 1918
Vzfw. _____ Sporbert	*in einer Flieger-Formation*	October 13, 1918
Vzfw. _____ Krüger	*in einer Flieger-Formation*	October 13, 1918

Sources: Awards through May 20, 1917: *"Sachsen in grosser Zeit - Band I"*
Awards after May 20, 1917: *"Ehren-Liste der Inhaber der Sächs. Silbernen Militär-St.-Heinrichs-Medaille 1914-1918"* - Hans Eichon, Friedrichshafen, 1989

[1.] The dates given are those listed in the two sources mentioned above. They are not the official bestowal dates of the awards which were from several weeks to several months earlier.

[2.] Possibly *Flieger-Abteilung (A)270.*

[3.] Possibly *Flieger-Abteilung 1.*

[4.] Possibly *Flieger-Abteilung 32,* but see Page 104.

[5.] An *Unteroffizier* Schulz of *Flieger-Abteilung 25* was cited for a raid on the Eastern Front over the evening of March 4 and 5, 1917. *Vizefeldwebel* Fritz Schulz of *Flieger-Abteilung (A)233* was killed on the Western Front on July 13, 1917.

Appendix XV

The First German Air Victory

Memoirs of a War Pilot by Richard Flashar

"On November 7, 1914, the following appeared in the 1st Army Daily Report:

'On November 5, 1914, *Oberleutnant* Demuth, in a plane piloted by *Leutnant* Flashar, shot down a French aircraft on our side of the lines. For their victorious air battle I express my recognition to both men.'

Signed: von Kluck."

These are the details of the incident:

On the morning of November 5, 1914, my observer, *Oberleutnant* Demuth, and I were given a long range reconnaissance mission for the area around Maux by the mounted field hunting corps. We had warm, pleasant weather.

We reached our objective on schedule. From 2,000 meters (planes at that time could go no higher) my 'Franz' - as observers are still nicknamed today - noted the road and rail traffic.

After a three hour flight, we returned to our own lines. I headed for our airfield, Loire Farm near Coney-le-Chateau, when I heard a knocking sound. This knocking repeated itself and still another time. Disturbed, I looked over the plane. The engine was still running at full power.

I looked around again to see if something was wrong with the rudder. But what did I find! Barely two plane lengths to the rear and at the same altitude was a French aircraft of the 'Parasol' type, a high winger. I saw the big blue/white/red cockade, the faces of the crew, one with a carbine shooting at us with an unobstructed view. That was the knocking sound I couldn't identify before. I still wonder to this day how the French 'Franz' wasn't able to shoot us down.

At that time pilots were not experienced in air battle. Naturally, I immediately banked to get out of the line of fire. This alerted Demuth but when we straightened out, the Frenchman was still directly behind us.

Demuth grabbed his rapid fire rifle and let off a string of shots. When I turned around, the Frenchman was gone. Thereupon I immediately landed. Below we received a huge welcome. They had seen everything from the field and figured our lives were no long worth one red cent. The Frenchman lay three kilometers away destroyed, the engine buried a half meter into the ground. This was the first air victory in the war that was recognized by *Kogenluft*.

A wealthy Cologne citizen, motivated by the many air victories of Boelcke and Immelmann, told the High Command in 1916 that he wanted to donate a stipend to fliers who shot down their first enemy plane in air battle.

The High Command (*Kogenluft* = *KOmmandierende GENeral der LUFTstreitkräfte*) thanked the donor but said that a monetary gift to soldiers was out of the question. It was suggested that a donation be made to help the dependants of fliers who had fallen. The two officers (in question) would receive an honorary gift from the Inspectorate of Aviation.

At Christmas 1916, I received a gold watch from the Inspectorate of Aviation with the inscription: 'To *Oberleutnant* Flashar, Pilot of the First Victorious German Aircraft, on 5 November 1914. The Inspectorate of Aviation.' "

Selected Bibliography

Official Documents

Flieger-Formationen, Teil 10, Luftstreitkräfte, Abschnitt B. Berlin, 1918

Militär-Wochenblatt, veröffentlichte preussische Ordens-Verleihungen 1914-1918

Nachrichtenblatt der Luftstreitkräfte, Feb. 18, 1917 - Oct. 22, 1918

Royal Flying Corps/Royal Air Force Casualty Lists, Jan. 1, 1916 - Nov. 24, 1918

Royal Flying Corps/Royal Air Force Communiques, July 27, 1915 - Nov. 11, 1918

War Diary or Intelligence Summary, Royal Flying Corps/Royal Air Force, Nov. 1, 1915 - Dec. 31, 1918

Unofficial Documents

Ruhmesblätter der deutschen fliegertruppe, 1914 - 1918

Books and Periodicals

Blondel, Jean-Michel, *Ordres des États de L'Allemagne Impériale, Orders of the Imperial German States,* 1987

Bodenschatz, Karl, *Jagd in Flandern Himmel,* Munich, 1935

Boelcke, Oswald, *An Aviator's Field Book* (translated by Robert R. Hirsch), Nashville, 1991

Bowen, E.V., *The Prussian and German Iron Cross,* Colchester, 1986

Brinkmann, Jürgen, *Die Ritter des Ordens "Pour le Mérite" 1914 - 1918,* Hannover, 1982

Buchholtz, Hans-Georg, *Der Flieger Thom,* Königsberg, 1937

Buckler, Julius, *Malaula!* Berlin, 1939

Buddecke, Hans-Joachim, *El Schahin (der Jagdfalke),* Berlin, 1918

Carr, William, *A History of Germany 1815 - 1985, 3rd Edition,* New York, 1987

Cole, Christopher, *Royal Air Force Communiques 1918,* London, 1990

Cole, Christopher, *Royal Flying Corps Communiques 1915 - 1916,* London, 1990

Cole, Christopher and Cheesmen, E.F., *The Air Defence of Britain 1914 - 1918,* London, 1984

Eberhardt, Walter von, *Unsere Luftstreitkräfte 1914 - 18,* Berlin, 1940

Edkins, David, *The Prussian Orden Pour le Mérite,* Falls Church, 1981

Ferko, A.E., *Fliegertruppe 1914 - 1918,* Salem, 1980

_____, *Fliegertruppe 1914 - 1918 Nr. 2,* Salem, 1987

Fischer, Bruno, *Ehrenbuch des ordens vom Militär-Verdienst-Kreuz e. V.,* Berlin, 1960

Flugsport, various issues, Jan. 7, 1914 - December 24, 1919, Frankfurt a. Main

Geile, Willi, *Im Marineverordnungsblatt,* Hagen, 1989

_____, *Im Militär-Wochenblatt April 1914 bis November 1918,* Hagen, 1985

Gengler, Ludwig F., *Kampfflieger Rudolf Berthold,* Berlin, 1934

Gilbert, Martin, *First World War Atlas,* London, 1970

Goote, Thor, *In Trichtern und Wolken,* Brunswick, Berlin, Hamburg, 1934

Gray, Peter and Thetford, Owen, *German Aircraft of the First World War,* London, 1978

Gritzner, Maximilian, *Handbuch der Ritter-und Verdienstorden,* Graz, 1962

Grosz, Peter M. and Haddow, G.W., *The German Giants,* London, 1962 and 1988

Haller, Hanns, *Der Flieger von Rottenburg,* Bayreuth, 1939

Hamelman, William E., *The History of the Prussian Pour le Mérite Order, 1888-1918,* Dallas, 1985

Hayward, J.B., *The Times Diary and Index of the War, 1914 - 1918,* London, 1985

Hessenthal, Dr. Waldemar Hesse Edken von and Schreiber, Georg, *Die Ehrenzeichen des Deutsches Reiches,* Berlin, 1940

Hottenroth, Johann E., *Sachsen in grosser Zeit, Band I,* Leipzig, 1919

_____, *Sachsen in grosser Zeit, Band II,* Leipzig, 1919

_____, *Sachsen in grosser Zeit, Band III,* Leipzig, 1919

Hyronimus, Joseph, *Bayerns Goldenes Ehrenbuch,* Munich, 1928

Immelmann, Franz, *Max Immelmann "The Eagle of* Lille," (translated by Claud W. Sykes), London, no date

Imrie, Alex, *Fokker Fighters of World War One,* London, 1986

_____, *German Air Aces of World War One,* Poole, 1987

_____, *German Bombers of World War One,* London, 1990

_____, *German Fighter Units 1914 - May 1917,* London, 1978

_____, *German Fighter Units June 1917 - 1918,* London, 1978

_____, *German Naval Air Service,* London, 1989

_____, *Pictorial History of the German Army Air Service,* Chicago, 1973

Klietmann, Dr. K.-G., *Pour le Mérite und Tapferkeitsmedaille,* Berlin, 1966

Marshall, S.L.A., *World War I,* New York, 1985

Mertens, Dr. Emil, *Aus Deutschlands Grosser Zeit, Ehemals preussische Truppenteile: Flieger-Abteilung (A)235,* Thuringen, 1928

Mittler, E.S., *Ehren Rangliste des Ehemaligen Deutschen Heeres,* Berlin, 1926

_____, *Rangliste des activen Dienststandes der königlich Preussischen Armee und des XIII.(königlich Württembergischen) Armeekorps,* Berlin, 1914

_____, *Rangliste des Deutschen Reichsheeres, 1924 - 1932,* Berlin, 1924 - 1932

_____, *Rangliste (Dienstaltersliste) der Kaiserlich Deutschen Marine für das Jahr 1916,* Berlin, 1916

_____, *Rangliste (Dienstaltersliste) der Kaiserlich Deutschen Marine für das Jahr 1918,* Berlin, 1918

Möller, Hanns, *Geschichte Der Ritter Des Ordens Pour le Mérite Im Weltkrieg, Band I,* Berlin, 1935

_____, *Geschichte Der Ritter Des Ordens Pour le Mérite Im Weltkrieg, Band II,* Berlin, 1935

_____, *Kampf und Sieg eines Jagdgeschwaders,* Berlin, 1939

Morrow, John H., Jr., *German Air Power in World War I,* Lincoln, 1982

Musciano, Walter A., *Eagles of the Black Cross,* New York, 1965

Neumann, Georg P., *In der Luft unbesiegt,* Munich, 1923

Neville, D. G., *Medal Ribbons & Orders of Imperial Germany & Austria,* St. Ives, 1974

Nickel, Dr. B., *Kampfberichte von Inhabern des Preussischen Goldenen Militär-Verdienstkreuzez - Band 104,* Berlin, 1937

Nimmergut, Jörg, *Bänderkatalog Orden & Ehrenzeichen Deutschland 1800 - 1945,* Munich, 1991

_____, *Deutschland-Katalog 1991/92 Orden & Ehrenzeichen 1880 - 1945, 8. Jahrgang,* Munich, 1977

Nowarra, Heinz J., *Eisernes Kreuz und Balken Kreuz,* Mainz, 1968

_____ and Brown, Kimbrough S., *Von Richthofen and the Flying Circus,* Fallbrook, 1958

O'Connor, Neal W., *Aviation Awards of Imperial Germany in World War I - Volume I, Aviation Awards of the Kingdom of Bavaria,* Princeton, 1988

_____, *Aviation Awards of Imperial Germany in World War I and the Men Who Earned Them - Volume II, Aviation Awards of the Kingdom of Prussia,* Princeton, 1990

Ophaus, Franz-Josef, *Das Preussische Goldene Militär-Verdienst-Kreuz,* Berlin, 1936

Patzwall, Klaus D., *Das Preussische Goldene Militär-Verdienst-Kreuz, Band 2,* 1986

Pechmann, Dr. Günther Freiherr von, *Virtuti Pro Patria - Der königlich Bayerische Militär-Max-Josef-Orden,* Munich, 1966

Pflanze, Otto, *Bismarck and the Development of Germany, Volume I,* Princeton, 1990

_____, *Bismarck and the Development of Germany, Volume II,* Princeton, 1990

_____, *Bismarck and the Development of Germany, Volume III,* Princeton, 1990

Purves, Alec A., *The Medals, Decorations & Orders of the Great War 1914 - 1918,* London, 1975

Raff, Diether, *A History of Germany from the Medieval Empire to the Present,* New York, 1988

Raleigh, Walter and Jones, H.A., *The War in the Air, Volumes 1 - 5,* London, 1922-1938

Reschke, Horst A., *German Military Records as Genealogical Sources,* Salt Lake City, 1990

Richter, Georg, *Der Königlich Sächsische Militär-St. Heinrichs-Orden 1736 - 1918,* Frankfurt a. Main, 1964

Richthofen, Manfred Freiherr von, *Der rote Kampfflieger,* Berlin, 1917

Rimell, Raymond L., *Air War Over Great Britain 1914 - 1918,* Poole, 1987

_____, *The German Army Air Service in World War One,* London, 1985

Robertson, Bruce and other authors, *Air Aces of the 1914 - 1918,* Fallbrook, 1964

Roeingh, Rolf, *Zwei Generationen Luftwaffe,* Berlin, 1942

mit Brillanten - with Brilliants (real or paste
   stones embellishing insignia)
mit Eichenlaub - with Oakleaf
mit der Krone - with Crown
mit Schwertern - with Swords
mit Schwertern am Ringe - with Swords-on-Ring
ohne Schwertern - without Swords
Nachrichtenblatt - Intelligence Journal
Oesterreich - Austria
Offizier zur besonderen Verwendung - Officer
   attached for special duties, or Adjutant
Ordenskissen - Orders cushion (for displaying
   awards at a military funeral)
Prinz - Prince
Rangliste - Rank List
Ritter - Knight
Ritterkreuz - Knight's Cross
Ruhmesblätter - Leaves (or Pages) of Glory
Seeflugstation - Naval aviation station

Schloss - Castle
Spartakist - Left-wing German revolutionary
   movement after the Armistice. Named after
   the gladiator, Spartacus, who led a slave revolt
   against Rome and was killed in 71 B.C.
Staatsarchiv - State Archive
Stern - Star
Steuermann - Helmsman
Stufe - Degree
Turkei - Turkey
Übung - Training
Ungarn - Hungary
Walfisch - Whale
zur Landung gezwungen - Forced to land

Other Terms (French)

Chevalier - Knight
M.S. - Morane Saulnier

INDEX OF NAMES IN MAIN TEXT